Amazon SimpleDB Developer Guide

Scale your application's database on the cloud using Amazon SimpleDB

Prabhakar Chaganti

Rich Helms

BIRMINGHAM - MUMBAI

Amazon SimpleDB Developer Guide

First published: June 2010

Production Reference: 2240510

Published by Packt Publishing Ltd.
32 Lincoln Road
Olton
Birmingham, B27 6PA, UK.

ISBN 978-1-847197-34-4

www.packtpub.com

Cover Image by Tina Negus (tina_manthorpe@sky.com)

Credits

Authors
Prabhakar Chaganti
Rich Helms

Reviewers
Deepak Anupalli
Anders Samuelsson
Ashley Tate

Acquisition Editor
James Lumsden

Development Editors
Dhwani Devater
Reshma Sundaresan

Technical Editor
Ishita Dhabalia

Indexer
Monica Ajmera Mehta

Editorial Team Leader
Gagandeep Singh

Project Team Leader
Lata Basantani

Project Coordinator
Joel Goveya

Proofreader
Lynda Silwoski

Graphics
Nilesh Mohite

Production Coordinator
Adline Swetha Jesuthas

Cover Work
Adline Swetha Jesuthas

Foreword

Most software developers who work on the Internet love change. Change presents a new challenge, a new paradigm, and new technologies to learn. To realize this, all you have to do is look at the evolution of computers. During the 70s, we worked in a world of mainframes and raised floors. Only special people got to touch the computer, while others had to be content watching from outside of the fishbowl.

The 80s brought the mini-computer with dedicated CRT terminals. You could show data on the screen in any color as long as it was green, but the computer was down the hall in the back room. The 80s also introduced the personal computer. As PC power grew, the mini was replaced with the LAN-connected PC.

The 90s saw the advent of the Internet, and people dialed in, and in the early 2000s, the Internet went viral. As high-speed connections became common, the Internet replaced corporate networks. Computers went from rooms to luggables to "in my briefcase" to "in my pocket."

In 2010, we are seeing the growth of cloud computing. Selecting a brand and model of server computer is being replaced with renting a virtual server at a hosting service like Amazon. The purchaser of these virtual servers doesn't have to select a hardware "brand." I no more care about the brand of computer than I would care about what brand of pipe the water utility used to connect to my house. All I am buying is cycles and reliability.

This move to virtual servers also changes the capital required to propose the next viral application. I don't need to buy a large database cluster, hoping for the acceptance to fill it. I am billed for usage, not capacity. SimpleDB is one of those virtual offerings and the topic of this book.

Rich Helms

About the Authors

Prabhakar Chaganti is the founder and CTO of Ylastic, a startup that is building a single unified interface to architect, manage, and monitor a user's entire AWS Cloud computing environment: EC2, S3, RDS, AutoScaling, ELB, Cloudwatch, SQS, and SimpleDB. He is the author of *Xen Virtualization* and *GWT Java AJAX Programming*, both by Packt Publishing, and is also the winner of the community choice award for the most innovative virtual appliance in the VMware Global Virtual Appliance Challenge. He hangs out on Twitter as @pchaganti.

"It's never been done" is a call to action for **Rich Helms**. He has built a career on breaking new ground in the computer field. He developed CARES (Computer Assisted Recovery Enhancement System) for the Metropolitan Toronto Police in Canada. CARES was the first computer system in the world for aging missing children. CARES has been internationally recognized as pioneering work in child aging. Rich has also created several generations of e-learning platforms including Learn it script and most recently Educate Press.

Rich can be reached at `http://webmasterinresidence.ca`.

Rich is a seasoned software developer with over 30 years of experience. He spent 22 years in various positions at IBM including Chief Image Technology Architect. His credentials range from deep technical work (five patents in hardware and software) to running multinational R&D.

About the Reviewers

Deepak Anupalli is Architect for the Server Engineering group at Pramati Technologies. He has deep insight into various Java/J2EE technologies. He represents Pramati on the EJB and JPA expert groups and has led the Java EE 5 certification effort of Pramati Server. He is currently leading the effort to build a standards-based web-scale Application server. He is a visiting faculty member with IIIT-Hyderabad for a course on middleware and also speaks at various technology conferences. He holds a graduate degree in Computer Science and Engineering from National Institute of Technology (NIT Warangal, India).

Anders Samuelsson has over 25 years of experience in the computing industry. The main focus during this time has been with computer security. He currently works for Amazon.com with Amazon Web Services.

> I'd like to thank my wife Malena and my son Daniel and daughter Ida, for always standing by me and allowing me to spend time helping out with this book. I love you forever.

Ashley Tate is the founder of Coditate Software and the creator of Simple Savant, an advanced C# interface to SimpleDB. He is currently working on GridRoom, an application for collaborative sports-video review built on several Amazon Web Services, including SimpleDB. He lives near Atlanta with his wife and four children. You can find him online at `http://blog.coditate.com`.

I would like to dedicate this book to my brother Madhukar, who gave us all a big scare, and with typical panache came out of it stronger than ever, my sister-in-law Meghna for putting the rock of Gibraltar to shame and showing us all how to handle and deal with adversity, and my nephew Yuv, the two year old fire cracker. My two daughters Anika and Anya were understanding and patient beyond their years as I stuck to my Mac at all kinds of weird hours. Above all, this book would not have made it into the station without the constant support, love and encouragement from my lovely wife Nitika!

Prabhakar Chaganti

A special thanks to Dorothea, Mike, Mary, our little girl Margaret, and the gang at WCDR.

Rich Helms

Table of Contents

Preface

SimpleDB is a highly scalable, simple-to-use, and inexpensive database in the cloud from Amazon Web Services. But in order to use SimpleDB, you really have to change your mindset. This isn't a traditional relational database; in fact it's not relational at all. For developers who have experience working with relational databases, this may lead to misconceptions as to how SimpleDB works.

This practical book aims to address your preconceptions on how SimpleDB will work for you. You will be led quickly through the differences between relational databases and SimpleDB, and the implications of using SimpleDB. Throughout this book, there is an emphasis on demonstrating key concepts with practical examples for Java, PHP, and Python developers.

You will be introduced to this massively scalable schema less key-value data store: what it is, how it works, and why it is such a game changer. You will then explore the basic functionality offered by SimpleDB including querying, code samples, and a lot more. This book will help you deploy services outside the Amazon cloud and access them from any web host.

You will see how SimpleDB gives you the freedom to focus on application development. As you work through this book you will be able to optimize the performance of your applications using parallel operations, caching with memcache, asynchronous operations, and more.

Gain in-depth understanding of Amazon SimpleDB with PHP, Java, and Python examples, and run optimized database-backed applications on Amazon's Web Services cloud.

What this book covers

Chapter 1, Getting to Know SimpleDB, explores SimpleDB and the advantages of utilizing it to build web-scale applications.

Chapter 2, Getting Started with SimpleDB, moves on to set up an AWS account, enable SimpleDB service for the account, and install and set up libraries for Java, PHP, and Python. It also illustrates several SimpleDB operations using these libraries.

Chapter 3, SimpleDB versus RDBMS, sheds light on the differences between SimpleDB and a traditional RDBMS, as well as the pros and cons of using SimpleDB as the storage engine in your application.

Chapter 4, The SimpleDB Data Model, takes a detailed look at the SimpleDB data model and different methods for interacting with a domain, its items, and their attributes. It further talks about the domain metadata and reviews the various constraints imposed by SimpleDB on domains, items, and attributes.

Chapter 5, Data Types, discusses the techniques needed for storing different data types in SimpleDB, and explores a technique for storing numbers, Boolean values, and dates. It also teaches you about XML-restricted characters and encoding them using base64 encoding.

Chapter 6, Querying, describes the Select syntax for retrieving results from SimpleDB, and looks at the various operators and how to create predicates that allow you to get back the information you need.

Chapter 7, Storing Data on S3, introduces you to Amazon S3 and its use for storing large files. It practically modifies a sample domain to add additional metadata including a file key that is again used for naming the MP3 file uploaded to S3. The example used in this chapter shows you a simple way to store metadata on SimpleDB while storing associated content that is in the form of binary files on Amazon S3.

Chapter 8, Tuning and Usage Costs, mainly covers the BoxUsage of different SimpleDB queries and the usage costs, along with viewing the usage activity reports.

Chapter 9, Caching, explains memcached and Cache_Lite in detail and their use for caching. It further explores a way you can use memcached with SimpleDB to avoid making unnecessary requests to SimpleDB, that is, by using libraries in Java, PHP, and Python.

Chapter 10, Parallel Processing, analyzes how to utilize multiple threads for running parallel operations against SimpleDB in Java, PHP, and Python in order to speed up processing times and taking advantage of the excellent support for concurrency in SimpleDB.

What you need for this book

To get started with the book and try out the code samples included here you will need following software:

For Python:

- Python 2.5 (`http://python.org/download/`)
- Boto latest version (`http://code.google.com/p/boto/downloads/list`)

For Java:

- JDK6 latest version (`http://java.sun.com/javase/downloads/index.jsp`)
- Typica latest version (`http://typica.googlecode.com/files/typica-1.6.zip`)

For the PHP part:

- PHP with curl support enabled
- GeSHi (optional): If Generic Syntax Highlighter package is installed the PHP source will be formatted when displayed in the samples available free from `http://qbnz.com/highlighter/`

Who this book is for

If you are a developer wanting to build scalable, web-based database applications using SimpleDB, then this book is for you. You do not need to know anything about SimpleDB to read and learn from this book, and no basic knowledge is strictly necessary. This guide will help you to start from scratch and build advanced applications.

Conventions

In this book, you will find a number of styles of text that distinguish between different kinds of information. Here are some examples of these styles, and an explanation of their meaning.

Code words in text are shown as follows: "Typica provides a simple way to access the BoxUsage value along with the `RequestId`, when you query SimpleDB."

A block of code is set as follows:

```
public static void main(String[] args) {
    SimpleDB sdb = new SimpleDB(awsAccessId, awsSecretKey, true);
    try {
        ListDomainsResult domainsResult = sdb.listDomains();
        System.out.println("RequestID : "
            + domainsResult.getRequestId());
        System.out.println("Box Usage : "
            + domainsResult.getBoxUsage());
    } catch (SDBException ex) {
        System.out.println(ex.getMessage());
    }
}
```

When we wish to draw your attention to a particular part of a code block, the relevant lines or items are set in bold:

```
"Statement":[{
    "Effect":"Allow",
    "Action":"sdb:*",
    "Resource":"arn:aws:sdb:*:123456789012:domain/user*"
    "Condition":{
        "IpAddress":{
            "aws:SourceIp":"192.168.176.0/24"
        }
        "Bool":{
            "aws:SecureTransport":"true"
        }
    }
}
]
```

Any command-line input or output is written as follows:

```
memcached -p 12312 -d
```

New terms and **important words** are shown in bold. Words that you see on the screen, in menus or dialog boxes for example, appear in the text like this: "clicking the **Next** button moves you to the next screen".

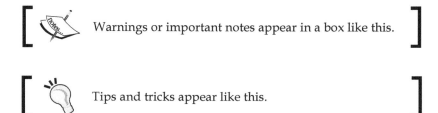

Warnings or important notes appear in a box like this.

Tips and tricks appear like this.

Reader feedback

Feedback from our readers is always welcome. Let us know what you think about this book—what you liked or may have disliked. Reader feedback is important for us to develop titles that you really get the most out of.

To send us general feedback, simply send an e-mail to feedback@packtpub.com, and mention the book title via the subject of your message.

If there is a book that you need and would like to see us publish, please send us a note in the **SUGGEST A TITLE** form on www.packtpub.com or e-mail suggest@packtpub.com.

If there is a topic that you have expertise in and you are interested in either writing or contributing to a book on, see our author guide on www.packtpub.com/authors.

Customer support

Now that you are the proud owner of a Packt book, we have a number of things to help you to get the most from your purchase.

Downloading the example code for the book

Visit https://www.packtpub.com//sites/default/files/downloads/7344_Code.zip to directly download the example code.

The downloadable files contain instructions on how to use them.

Errata

Although we have taken every care to ensure the accuracy of our content, mistakes do happen. If you find a mistake in one of our books—maybe a mistake in the text or the code—we would be grateful if you would report this to us. By doing so, you can save other readers from frustration, and help us to improve subsequent versions of this book. If you find any errata, please report them by visiting http://www.packtpub.com/support, selecting your book, clicking on the **let us know** link, and entering the details of your errata. Once your errata are verified, your submission will be accepted and the errata added to any list of existing errata. Any existing errata can be viewed by selecting your title from http://www.packtpub.com/support.

Piracy

Piracy of copyright material on the Internet is an ongoing problem across all media. At Packt, we take the protection of our copyright and licenses very seriously. If you come across any illegal copies of our works, in any form, on the Internet, please provide us with the location address or web site name immediately so that we can pursue a remedy.

Please contact us at copyright@packtpub.com with a link to the suspected pirated material.

We appreciate your help in protecting our authors, and our ability to bring you valuable content.

Questions

You can contact us at questions@packtpub.com if you are having a problem with any aspect of the book, and we will do our best to address it.

1
Getting to Know SimpleDB

Most developers would describe a modern database as relational with stored procedures and cross-table functions such as join. So why would you use a database that has none of these capabilities? The answer is scalability.

This morning, CNN ran a story on your new web application. Yesterday you had 10 concurrent users, and now your site is viral with 50,000 users signing on. Which database will handle 50,000 concurrent users without a complex expensive cluster? The answer is SimpleDB.

Why SimpleDB?

- Scalability
- Pay only for your use
- Access from any web-based system
- No fixed schema

Challenges?

- New metaphor — write seldom, read many
- Eventual consistency

SimpleDB is one of the core Amazon Web Services, which include **Amazon Simple Storage Service (S3)** and **Amazon Elastic Compute Cloud (EC2)**. Amazon SimpleDB stores your structured data as key-value pairs in the **Amazon Web Services (AWS)** cloud and lets you run real-time queries against this data. You can scale it easily in response to increased load from your successful applications without the need for a costly cluster database server complex.

SimpleDB, as illustrated in the following diagram, is designed to be used either as an independent data storage component in your applications or in conjunction with some of the other services from Amazon's stable of Cloud Services, such as Amazon S3 and Amazon EC2.

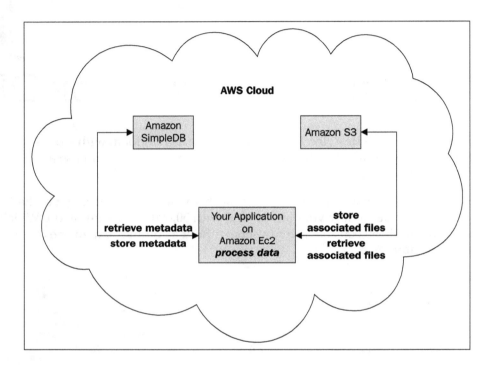

The biggest challenge in SimpleDB is learning to think in its unique metaphor. Like speaking a new language, you need to stop translating and start thinking in that language. Rather than thinking of SimpleDB as a database, approach it as a spreadsheet with some XML characteristics.

SimpleDB functionality can be accessed from almost any programming language (such as Python, Ruby, Java, PHP, Erlang, and Perl) using super simple HTTP-based requests. You can get started anytime you like, and you pay for it based on how much you use it. It is very different from a relational database, and takes a completely different approach toward storing and querying data. It follows the convention of **eventual consistency**. Think of it as a single master database for updates and a large collection of read database slaves. Any changes made to your data will need to be propagated across all the different copies. This can sometimes take a few seconds depending upon the system load at that time and network latency, which means that a consumer of your domain and data may not see the changes immediately. The changes will eventually be propagated throughout SimpleDB, but this is an important consideration you need to think about when designing your application.

Experimenting with SimpleDB

As SimpleDB is so different, it helps to have a tool for manipulating and exploring the database. When developing with a MySQL database, phpMyAdmin allows the developer to work directly on the database. SimpleDB has a similar free Firefox plugin called **sdbtool** (http://code.google.com/p/sdbtool/). Another Firefox plugin used in the more advanced examples is S3Fox (http://www.s3fox.net/) for administering the Amazon S3 storage. In this book, we cover several basic sample applications. We have also provided code to show each SimpleDB application using three languages: Java, PHP, and Python.

As access to SimpleDB can be from any site on the Web, the PHP samples can be downloaded and run directly from your site. To run any sample, an Amazon account is required. These samples let you explore most of the SimpleDB API, as well as some of the S3 API capabilities.

You can both download and try the PHP samples from http://www.webmasterinresidence.ca/simpledb/.

How does SimpleDB work?

The best way to wrap your head around the way SimpleDB works is to picture a spreadsheet that contains your structured data. For instance, a contact database that stores information on your customers can be represented in SimpleDB as follows:

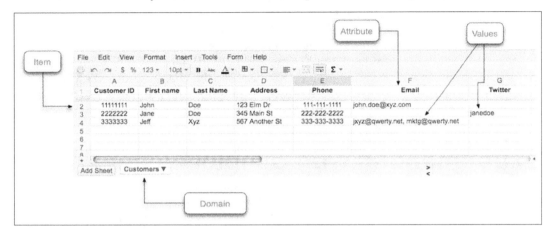

As SimpleDB is a different database metaphor, new terms have been introduced. The use of this new terminology by Amazon stresses that the traditional assumptions may not be valid.

Domain

The entire customers table will be represented as the domain **Customers**. Domains group similar data for your application, and you can have up to 100 domains per AWS account. If required, you can increase this limit further by filling out a form on the SimpleDB website. The data stored in these domains is retrieved by making queries against the specific domain. There is no concept of **joins** as in the relational database world; therefore, queries run within a specific domain and not across domains.

Item

Each customer is represented by a unique Customer ID. Items are similar to rows in a database table. Each item identifies a single object and contains data for that individual item as a number of key-value attributes. Each item is identified by a unique key or identifier, or in traditional terminology, the primary key. SimpleDB does not support the concept of auto-incrementing keys, and most people use a generated key such as the unix timestamp combined with the user identifier or something similar as the unique identifier for an item. You can have up to one billion items in each domain.

Attributes

Each customer item will have distinguishing characteristics that are represented by an attribute. A customer will have a name, a phone number, an address, and other such attributes, which are similar to the columns in a table in a database. SimpleDB even enables you to have different attributes for each item in a domain. This kind of schema independence lets you mix and match items within a domain to satisfy the needs of your application easily, while at the same time enables you to take advantage of the benefits of the automatic indexing provided by SimpleDB. If your company suddenly decides to start marketing using Twitter, you can simply add a new attribute to your customer domain for the customers who have a Twitter ID! In traditional database terminology, there is no need to add a new column to the table.

Values

Each customer attribute will be associated with a value, which is the same as a cell in a spreadsheet or the value of a column in a database. A relational database or a spreadsheet supports only a single value for each cell or column, while SimpleDB allows you to have multiple values for a single attribute. This lets you do things such as store multiple e-mail addresses for a customer while taking advantage of automatic indexing, without the need for you to manually create new and separate columns for each e-mail address, and then index each new column. In a relational DB, a separate table with a join would be used to store the multiple values. Unlike a delimited list in a character field, the multiple values are indexed, enabling quick searching.

It is a simple way of modeling your data, but at the same time, it is different from a relational database model that is familiar to most users. The following table compares SimpleDB components with a spreadsheet and a relational database:

Relational Database	Spreadsheet	SimpleDB
Table	Worksheet	Domain
Row	Row	Item
Column	Cell	Attribute
Value	Value	Value(s)

How do I interact with SimpleDB?

You interact with SimpleDB by making authenticated HTTP requests along with the desired parameters. There are several libraries available in different programming languages that encapsulate this entire process and make it even easier to interact with SimpleDB by removing some of the tedium of manually constructing the HTTP requests. The next chapter explores these libraries and the advantages provided by them.

There are three main types of actions that you will need to do when you are working with SimpleDB—create, modify, and retrieve information about your domains by using the following operations:

- CreateDomain: Create a new domain that contains your dataset.
- DeleteDomain: Delete an existing domain.
- ListDomains: List all the domains.
- DomainMetadata: Retrieve information that gives you a general picture of the domain and the items that are stored within it, such as:
    ◦ The date and time the metadata was last updated
    ◦ The number of all items in the domain
    ◦ The number of attribute name/value pairs in the domain
    ◦ The number of unique attribute names in the domain
    ◦ The total size of all item names in the domain, in bytes
    ◦ The total size of all attribute values, in bytes
    ◦ The total size of all unique attribute names, in bytes

You can create or modify the data stored within your domains by using the following operations:

- PutAttributes: Create or update an item and its attributes. Items will automatically be indexed by SimpleDB as they are added.
- BatchPutAttributes: Create or update multiple attributes (up to 25) in a single call for improved overall throughput of bulk write operations.
- DeleteAttributes: Delete an item, an attribute, or an attribute value.

You can retrieve items that match your criteria from the dataset stored in your domains using the following operations:

- `GetAttributes`: Retrieve an item and all or a subset of its attributes and values matching your criteria.

- `Select`: Retrieve an item and all or a subset of its attributes and values matching your criteria, using the SELECT syntax that is popular in the SQL world.

The following diagram illustrates the different components of SimpleDB and the operations that can be used for interacting with them:

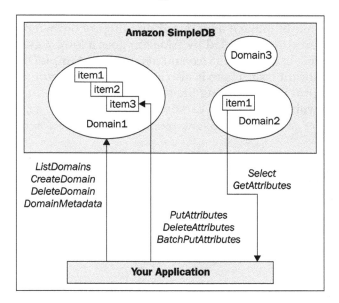

How is SimpleDB priced?

Amazon provides a free tier for SimpleDB along with pricing for usage above the free tier limit. The charges are based on the machine utilization of each SimpleDB request along with the amount of machine capacity that is utilized for completing the specified request normalized to the hourly capacity of a 1.7 GHz Xeon processor.

Free tier

As of the publication date of this book, there are no charges on the first 25 machine hours, 1 GB of data transfer, and 1 GB of storage that you consume every month. This is a significant amount of usage being provided for free for this limited time period by Amazon, and there are many kinds of applications that can operate entirely within this free tier. Pricing details are available at `http://aws.amazon.com/simpledb/`.

While a credit card is required to sign up, usage can be checked at any time with the Amazon Account Activity web page. Amazon estimates about 2,000,000 GET or SELECT API calls per month without any charge.

The pricing details might make it a bit daunting to figure out what your costs may be initially, but the free tier provided by Amazon goes a long way toward getting you more comfortable using the service and also putting SimpleDB through its paces without significant cost. There is also a nice calculator provided on the AWS site that is very helpful for computing the monthly usage costs for SimpleDB and the other Amazon web services. You can find the Amazon web services cost calculator at `http://calculator.s3.amazonaws.com/calc5.html`.

Why should I use SimpleDB?

You now have an overview of the service, and you are reasonably familiar with what SimpleDB can do. It is a great piece of technology that enables you to create scalable applications that are capable of using massive amounts of data, and you can put this power and simplicity to use in your own applications.

Make your applications simpler to architect

You can leverage SimpleDB in your applications to quickly add, edit, and retrieve data using a simple set of API calls. The well-thought-out API and simplicity of usage will make your applications easier to design, architect, and maintain in the long run, while removing the burdens of data modeling, index maintenance, and performance tuning.

Build flexibility into your applications

You no longer have to either know or pre-define every single piece of data that you will possibly "need to store" for your application. You expand your data set as you go and add the new attributes only when they are absolutely needed. SimpleDB enables you to do this easily, and even the indexing for these newly-added attributes is automatically handled behind the scenes without any need for your intervention.

Create high-performance web applications

High-performance web applications need the ability to store and retrieve data in a fast and efficient way. Amazon SimpleDB provides your applications with this ability while removing a lot of the administrative and maintenance complexities, leaving you free to focus on what's important to you — your application.

Take advantage of lower costs

You pay only for the SimpleDB resources that you actually consume, and you no longer need to lay out significant expenditures up front for database software licenses or even hardware. The capacity planning and handling of any spikes in load and traffic are automatically handled by Amazon, freeing valuable resources that can be deployed in other areas. SimpleDB pricing passes on to you the cost savings achieved by Amazon's economies of scale.

Scale your applications on demand

And last but most importantly, you can easily handle traffic and load spikes on your applications, as SimpleDB will be doing all of the heavy lifting and scaling for you. You can even handle the massive and tsunami-like increases in traffic that can result from being mentioned on the front page of Yahoo or Digg, or becoming a trendy topic on Twitter.

Architect for the cloud

SimpleDB is designed to integrate easily and work well with the other cloud services from Amazon such as Amazon EC2 and Amazon S3. This enables you to take full advantage of these other services and offload data processing and file storage needs to the cloud, while still using SimpleDB for your structured data storage needs. Web-scale computing for your application needs along with cost-effectiveness is easier thanks to these cloud services.

Summary

In this chapter, we explored SimpleDB and the advantages of utilizing it to build web-scale applications. In the next chapter, we will start interacting with SimpleDB, and getting familiar with creating and modifying datasets utilizing one of the widely available SimpleDB software libraries.

Getting Started with SimpleDB

In this chapter, we going to sign up for an AWS account, download and install the necessary libraries, and create little code snippets for exploring SimpleDB. We will introduce the libraries as well as the SimpleDB Firefox plugin for manipulating SimpleDB. We will also examine the two methods for accessing SimpleDB: SOAP and ReST. For PHP users we will introduce the PHP sample library. You can download and install the samples on your PHP5 server so that you can try the samples as you read about them.

Creating an AWS account

In order to start using SimpleDB, you will first need to sign up for an account with AWS.

Visit http://aws.amazon.com/ and click on **Create an AWS Account**.

You can sign up either by using your e-mail address for an existing Amazon account, or by creating a completely new account. You may wish to have multiple accounts to separate billing for projects. This could make it easier for you to track billing for separate accounts. After a successful signup, navigate to the main AWS page— http://aws.amazon.com/, and click on the **Your Account** link at any time to view your account information and make any changes to it if needed.

Enabling SimpleDB service for AWS account

Once you have successfully set up an AWS account, you must follow these steps to enable the SimpleDB service for your account:

1. Log in to your AWS account.

2. Navigate to the SimpleDB home page— http://aws.amazon.com/ simpledb/.

3. Click on the **Sign Up For Amazon SimpleDB** button on the right side of the page.

4. Provide the requested credit card information and complete the signup process.

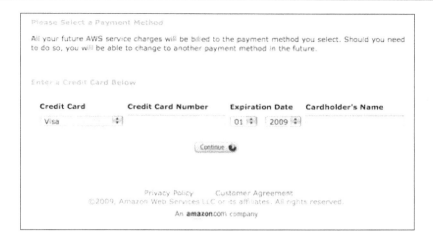

Please Select a Payment Method

All your future AWS service charges will be billed to the payment method you select. Should you need to do so, you will be able to change to another payment method in the future.

Enter a Credit Card Below

Credit Card	Credit Card Number	Expiration Date	Cardholder's Name
Visa		01 2009	

Continue

Privacy Policy   Customer Agreement
©2009, Amazon Web Services LLC or its affiliates. All rights reserved.
An amazon.com company

You have now successfully set up your AWS account and enabled it for SimpleDB.

All communication with SimpleDB or any of the Amazon web services must be through either the SOAP interface or the Query/ReST interface. The request messages sent through either of these interfaces is digitally signed by the sending user in order to ensure that the messages have not been tampered within transit, and that they really originate from the sending user. Requests that use the Query/ReST interface will use the access keys for signing the request, whereas requests to the SOAP interface will use the x.509 certificates.

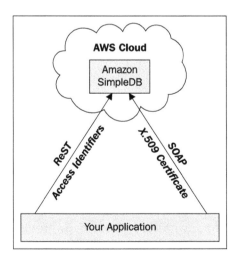

Your new AWS account is associated with the following items:

- A unique 12-digit AWS account number for identifying your account.

- AWS Access Credentials are used for the purpose of authenticating requests made by you through the ReST Request API to any of the web services provided by AWS. An initial set of keys is automatically generated for you by default. You can regenerate the Secret Access Key at any time if you like. Keep in mind that when you generate a new access key, all requests made using the old key will be rejected.

  - ° An Access Key ID identifies you as the person making requests to a web service.

  - ° A Secret Access Key is used to calculate the digital signature when you make requests to the web service.

  - ° Be careful with your Secret Access Key, as it provides full access to the account, including the ability to delete all of your data.

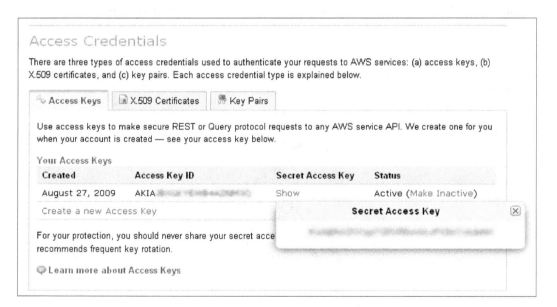

- All requests made to any of the web services provided by AWS using the SOAP protocol use the X.509 security certificate for authentication. There are no default certificates generated automatically for you by AWS. You must generate the certificate by clicking on the **Create a new Certificate** link, then download them to your computer and make them available to the machine that will be making requests to AWS.

- ○ Public and private key for the x.509 certificate. You can either upload your own x.509 certificate if you already have one, or you can just generate a new certificate and then download it to your computer.

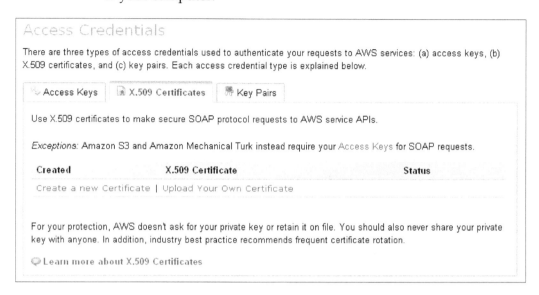

Query API and authentication

There are two interfaces to SimpleDB. The SOAP interface uses the SOAP protocol for the messages, while the ReST Requests uses HTTP requests with request parameters to describe the various SimpleDB methods and operations. In this book, we will be focusing on using the ReST Requests for talking to SimpleDB, as it is a much simpler protocol and utilizes straightforward HTTP-based requests and responses for communication, and the requests are sent to SimpleDB using either a HTTP GET or POST method.

The ReST Requests need to be authenticated in order to establish that they are originating from a valid SimpleDB user, and also for accounting and billing purposes. This authentication is performed using your access key identifiers. Every request to SimpleDB must contain a request signature calculated by constructing a string based on the Query API and then calculating an RFC 2104-compliant HMAC-SHA1 hash, using the Secret Access Key.

The basic steps in the authentication of a request by SimpleDB are:

- You construct a request to SimpleDB.

- You use your Secret Access Key to calculate the request signature, a Keyed-Hashing for **Message Authentication code (HMAC)** with an SHA1 hash function.

- You send the request data, the request signature, timestamp, and your Access Key ID to AWS.

- AWS uses the Access Key ID in the request to look up the associated Secret Access Key.

- AWS generates a request signature from the request data using the retrieved Secret Access Key and the same algorithm you used to calculate the signature in the request.

- If the signature generated by AWS matches the one you sent in the request, the request is considered to be authentic. If the signatures are different, the request is discarded, and AWS returns an error response. If the timestamp is older than 15 minutes, the request is rejected.

The procedure for constructing your requests is simple, but tedious and time consuming. This overview was intended to make you familiar with the entire process, but don't worry—you will not need to go through this laborious process every single time that you interact with SimpleDB. Instead, we will be leveraging one of the available libraries for communicating with SimpleDB, which encapsulates a lot of the repetitive stuff for us and makes it simple to dive straight into playing with and exploring SimpleDB!

SimpleDB libraries

There are libraries available for interacting with SimpleDB from a wide variety of languages. Most of these libraries provide support for all of the basic operations of SimpleDB. However, Amazon has been working hard to enhance and improve the functionality of SimpleDB, and as a result, they add new features frequently. You will want to leverage these new features as quickly as possible in your own applications. It is important that you select a library that has an active development cycle, so the new features are available fairly quickly after Amazon has released them. Another important consideration is the community around each library. An active community that uses the library ensures good quality and also provides a great way to get your questions answered. There are five libraries that meet all of these criteria:

- **Java Library for Amazon SimpleDB**: This is the official Java library provided by Amazon. In our experience, this library is a bit too verbose and requires a lot of boilerplate code.

- **Typica**: This is an open source Java library that provides access to all of the latest functionalities provided by SimpleDB. It is actively maintained and has a large community of users.

- **SDB-PHP and S3-PHP**: SDB-PHP is an open source PHP library that provides an easy ReST-based interface to Amazon's SimpleDB service (`http://sourceforge.net/projects/php-sdb/`), and S3-PHP is an open source PHP library to access S3-PHP (`http://undesigned.org.za/2007/10/22/amazon-s3-php-class`).

- **RightAWS**: An open source Ruby library for SimpleDB, which is quite popular with users who are building Ruby on Rails-based webapps that need SimpleDB functionality. It is actively maintained and has a large community of users.

- **Boto**: An open source Python library for SimpleDB. This is a comprehensive library that provides access to all of the SimpleDB features.

These are all great libraries, and they will be useful to you if your application is written in one of these languages. We will include samples in three of the languages—Java, PHP, and Python.

SDBtool — Firefox plugin

SDBtool is a Firefox plugin by Bizo Engineering for manipulating SimpleDB. As you go through the sample code, you can then view the results in the database. This is invaluable in both viewing results as well as updating or deleting data.

The program is a Firefox web browser (`http://www.mozilla.com/firefox/`) plugin. One of Firefox's key features is the ability to install plugins to expand the capabilities. Firefox is available for Microsoft Windows and Apple Mac OS X as well as Linux.

To install SDBtool, visit `http://code.google.com/p/SDBtool/` with a Firefox browser. Then click on the **Click here to install** link. Firefox will ask for a confirmation to install the plugin.

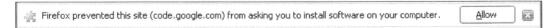

To start SDBtool, click on **Tools | SDB Tool** in the top menu.

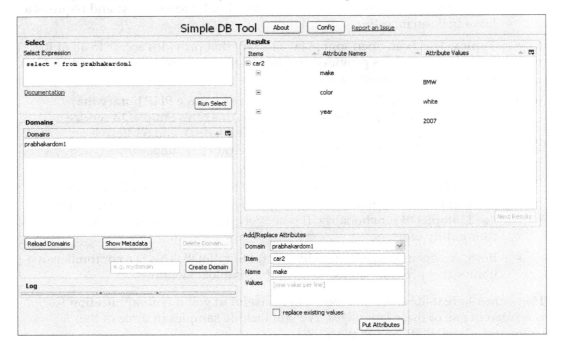

When SDBtool starts for the first time, it is necessary to configure your Access Keys. Click on the **Config** button and enter your Access Key and Secret Key. There is also a checkbox that sets if the tool can delete a domain. If you are working on a production database, it is wise to leave this unchecked.

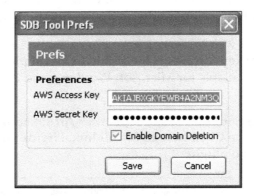

A connection to your SimpleDB database will open in a new browser tab. The list of available domains will be listed in the domain area.

The SDBtool screen is divided into four areas:

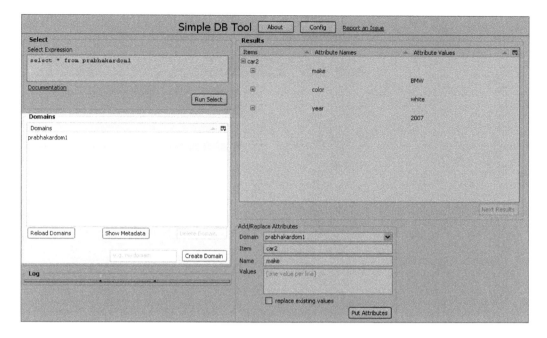

This area is used to create or display domains.

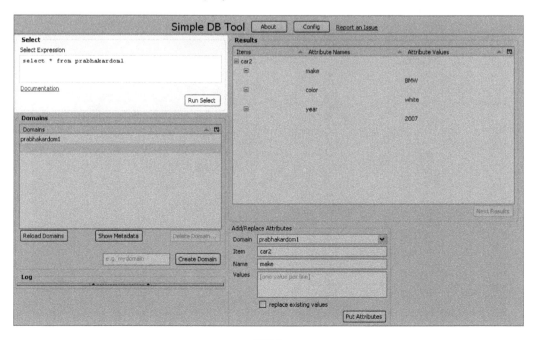

This area is used to write SQL queries.

We will cover the SQL syntax in *Chapter 6, Querying*. Until that time, use the simple `select * from domain_name` to view all items in a domain.

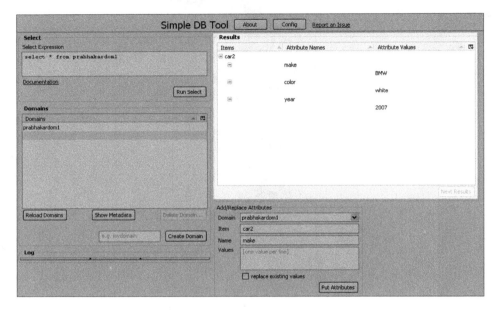

This area is used to display SQL query results.

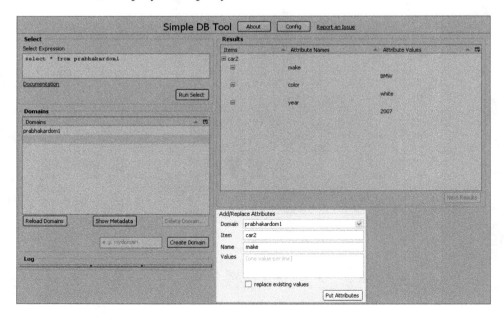

This area is used to add or replace attribute values.

Sample outline — performing basic operations

In this book, each sample set will begin with a sample outline. The sample goals, as well as common SimpleDB principles, will be introduced. Then the sample will break into three streams: Java, PHP, and Python.

The purpose of this sample is to introduce code snippets to create, list, and delete domains as well as create, query, and delete items.

Each domain is a container for storing items. Any item that does not have any attributes is considered empty and is automatically deleted by SimpleDB. You can therefore have empty domains stored in SimpleDB, but not items with zero attributes. Each value is stored as a UTF-8 string in SimpleDB. This is an important consideration, and you need to be aware of it when storing and querying different data types, such as numbers or dates. You must convert their data into an appropriate string format, so that your queries against the data return expected results. The conversion of data adds a little bit of extra work on your application side, but it also provides you with the flexibility to enforce data ReSTrictions at your application layer without the need for the data store to enforce the constraints. We will explore data types and their conversions to the appropriate string format in detail in *Chapter 5, Data Types*.

Basic operations with Java

Java is a very popular language used for building enterprise applications. In this section we will download **typica** and then use it for exploring SimpleDB.

Exploring SimpleDB with Java

Download **typica** from the project site at Google Code—http://code.google.com/p/typica/.

The latest version of **typica** at the time of writing this is 1.6. Download the ZIP file from the website. Unzip to the folder of your choice and add the typica.jar to your classpath. You also need some third-party libraries used by typica and can download each of these dependencies and add the corresponding JAR files to your classpath:

- commons-logging (http://commons.apache.org/downloads/download_logging.cgi)
- JAXB (https://jaxb.dev.java.net/servlets/ProjectDocumentList?folderID=6746&expandFolder=6746&folderID=3952)
- commons-httpclient (http://hc.apache.org/downloads.cgi)
- commons-codec (http://commons.apache.org/downloads/download_codec.cgi)

We are going to learn about and explore SimpleDB from Java by writing small snippets of Java code for interacting with it. Here is the skeleton of a Java class named **ExploreSdb** that contains a main method. We will add code to the main method, and you can run the class to see it in action from the console or in the IDE of your choice.

```
package simpledbbook;
public class ExploreSdb {
    public static void main(String[] args) {
        SimpleDB sdb = new SimpleDB(awsAccessId, awsSecretKey, true);
    }
}
```

In this class, we create a SimpleDB object from the class provided by typica. This will be our connection to Amazon SimpleDB and will be used for interacting with it. As we have discussed earlier, in order to use the API, we will need to specify the AWS keys. Typica lets you store the keys in a file named aws.properties, or you can explicitly provide them when you are creating a connection. In this chapter, we will use the explicit way. In each of the sections below, we will add snippets of code to the main() method.

Creating a domain with Java

A **SimpleDB domain** is a container for storing data, and is similar in concept to a
table in a relational database. You create a domain by calling the createDomain()
method and specifying a name for the domain.

```java
public static void main(String[] args) {
    SimpleDB sdb = new SimpleDB(awsAccessId, awsSecretKey, true);
    try {
        Domain domain = sdb.createDomain("cars");
    } catch (SDBException ex) {
        System.out.println(ex.getMessage());
    }
}
```

Listing domains with Java

You can display a list of domains by calling the listDomains() method. This will
return a list of domain objects.

```java
public static void main(String[] args) {
    SimpleDB sdb = new SimpleDB(awsAccessId, awsSecretKey, true);
    try {
        ListDomainsResult domainsResult = sdb.listDomains();
        List<Domain> domains = domainsResult.getDomainList();
        for (Domain dom : domains) {
            System.out.println("Domain : " + dom.getName());
        }
    } catch (SDBException ex) {
        System.out.println(ex.getMessage());
    }
}
```

Manipulating items with Java

We will now add some items to our newly-created domain. You create an item and
then specify its attributes as follows:

```java
public static void main(String[] args) {
    SimpleDB sdb = new SimpleDB(awsAccessId, awsSecretKey, true);
    try {
        Domain domain = sdb.getDomain("cars");
        Item item = domain.getItem("car1");
        List<ItemAttribute> list = new ArrayList<ItemAttribute>();
        list.add(new ItemAttribute("make", "BMW", false));
```

```
            list.add(new ItemAttribute("color", "grey", false));
            list.add(new ItemAttribute("year", "2008", false));
            list.add(new ItemAttribute("desc", "Sedan", false));
            list.add(new ItemAttribute("model", "530i", false));
            item.putAttributes(list);

            item = domain.getItem("car2");
            list = new ArrayList<ItemAttribute>();
            list.add(new ItemAttribute("make", "BMW", false));
            list.add(new ItemAttribute("color", "white", false));
            list.add(new ItemAttribute("year", "2007", false));
            list.add(new ItemAttribute("desc", "Sports Utility Vehicle",
                                        false));
            list.add(new ItemAttribute("model", "X5", false));
            item.putAttributes(list);
        } catch (SDBException ex) {
            System.out.println(ex.getMessage());
        }
    }
}
```

Now retrieve the items from the domain by using a simple SELECT query. We will discuss the SELECT syntax in detail later in *Chapter 6*.

```
    public static void main(String[] args) {
        SimpleDB sdb = new SimpleDB(awsAccessId, awsSecretKey, true);
        try {
            Domain domain = sdb.getDomain("cars");
            String queryString = "SELECT * FROM `cars`";
                int itemCount = 0;
                String nextToken = null;
                do {
                    QueryWithAttributesResult queryResults =
                        domain.selectItems(queryString, nextToken);
                    Map<String, List<ItemAttribute>> items =
                        queryResults.getItems();
                    for (String id : items.keySet()) {
                        System.out.println("Item : " + id);
                        for (ItemAttribute attr : items.get(id)) {
                            System.out.println(attr.getName() + " = "
                            + attr.getValue());
                        }
                        itemCount++;
                    }
                    nextToken = queryResults.getNextToken();
                } while (nextToken != null && !nextToken
                    .trim().equals(""));
```

```
    } catch (SDBException ex) {
        System.out.println(ex.getMessage());
    }
}
```

You can retrieve an individual item and its attributes by specifying the item name.

```
public static void main(String[] args) {
    SimpleDB sdb = new SimpleDB(awsAccessId, awsSecretKey, true);
    try {
        Domain domain = sdb.getDomain("cars");
        Item car1 = domain.getItem("car1");
        List<ItemAttribute> itemAttrs = car1.getAttributes();
        for (ItemAttribute attr : itemAttrs) {
            System.out.println(attr.getName()
            + " = " + attr.getValue());
        }
    } catch (SDBException ex) {
        System.out.println(ex.getMessage());
    }
}
```

Deleting a domain with Java

Finally, you can delete a domain by specifying its name. Once you delete a domain, the data is gone forever. So use caution when deleting a domain!

```
public static void main(String[] args) {
    SimpleDB sdb = new SimpleDB(awsAccessId, awsSecretKey, true);
    try {
        sdb.deleteDomain("cars");
    } catch (SDBException ex) {
        System.out.println(ex.getMessage());
    }
}
```

Basic operations with PHP

PHP is a popular scripting language for writing web applications. Many of the most popular open source applications such as WordPress are written with PHP. There are several SimpleDB APIs available. The PHP samples are based on an API written by Dan Myers. This program is easy to understand, use, and expand. Rich Helms has expanded the API and provided samples for this book.

All of the sample code can be downloaded and run from your site, or executed from our site, with your Access Keys to your SimpleDB. Note that the user interface in these samples is very basic. The focus is on illustrating the SimpleDB interface.

Exploring SimpleDB with PHP

Rich Helms: "When I wrote my first SimpleDB PHP program, I struggled to find a working sample to build on. After a number of APIs, I found Dan Myers' SDB-PHP. The entire API was in one file and simple to understand. Working with Dan, I expanded the API to provide complete SimpleDB functionality including data normalization. When I needed a PHP S3 API for backup/ReSTore of SimpleDB, I used S3-PHP by Donovan Schonknecht. SDB-PHP was based on S3-PHP".

Visit `http://www.webmasterinresidence.ca/simpledb/` to download the PHP sample package, which has the sample programs discussed in this book. All programs are complete and can be run unaltered on your server. The samples use PHP 5.

The menu (`index.php`) provides access to all samples. When a program is run, the source is shown below in a box. If the free package **Generic Syntax Highlighter (GeSHi)** is installed, the source will be formatted when displayed. To get GeSHi, go to `http://qbnz.com/highlighter/`.

SimpleDB PHP Sample Programs

Key/Secret Key
1. Set your key/secret key for the session
2. Destroy your key/secret session keys

Domains
3. List Domains and Domain Metadata
4. Create Sample domain 'car-s'
5. Delete Sample domain 'car-s'

Add Items
6. Create Multiple Records One at a Time in car-s
7. Create Multiple Records with batchPutAttributes in car-s

List Items
8. List All Sample Records in car-s
9. List All Sample Records with a NextToken car-s

Delete Items/Attributes
10. Delete 'car1' item from 'car-s'
11. Delete 'car3' item 'year' and one 'color' from 'car-s'

Data Normalization
12. Encode/Decode Numbers
13. Encode/Decode Dates
14. Encode/Decode Boolean
15. Encode/Decode Base64

Select
16. Create Songs Domain with Sample Items
17. Select Year='1985' from Songs
18. Try SQL Queries
19. Query all attributes for '112222222' Item
20. Delete domain 'songs'

Backup
21. Backup a Domain
22. Restore a Domain

S3
23. Upload MP3 Song to S3

API Code
24. Display 'sdb.php' and 'config.inc.php'
25. Display 'S3.php'

Download source files

Rich Helms rich@webmasterinresidence.ca

Source - index.php

```php
<?php require_once('config.inc.php'); ?>
<html><title>SimpleDB PHP Samples</title><body><h3>SimpleDB PHP Sample Programs</h3>

<ol>
<strong>Key/Secret Key</strong>
<li><a href=setkeys.php>Set your key/secret key for the session</a></li>
```

The samples are structured into groups: entering your Access Keys, domains, items, and attributes; data normalization, select, and S3; and backing up SimpleDB into S3. As you go through the programs, use the Firefox SDBtool plugin to examine the database and see the results.

Select the first menu item to set the keys.

Set SimpleDB Keys

Keys saved Return to Menu

Key: AKIA ████████████████

Secret Key: ●●●

[Set Keys for this session]

The keys are stored in two PHP session variables.

The Key and Secret Key values are stored in two session variables. Program `config.inc.php` reads the session variables to set two defined keys: `awsAccessKey` and `awsSecretKey`. If you are downloading and running the source from your site, you can just define the keys and avoid the session variables. Using session variables enables you to try the code at my location and still talk to your SimpleDB without me having access to your keys.

```
require_once('config.inc.php');
if (!empty($_POST["key"])) {
    $_SESSION['key'] = $_POST["key"];
}
if (!empty($_POST["secretkey"])) {
    $_SESSION['secretkey'] = $_POST["secretkey"];
}
```

The program calls itself passing the value of the input fields.

```
session_start();
if (!empty($_SESSION['key'])) $key = $_SESSION['key'];
if (!empty($_SESSION['secretkey'])) $secretkey =
    $_SESSION['secretkey'];
// if your own installation, just replace $key and $secretkey
//   with your values
if (!defined('awsAccessKey')) define('awsAccessKey', $key);
if (!defined('awsSecretKey')) define('awsSecretKey', $secretkey);
```

When the second menu item is selected, the session variables are destroyed.

```
require_once('config.inc.php');
session_destroy();
```

To access SimpleDB, first we create a connection. File `sdb.php` has the API functions.

```
require_once('config.inc.php');
if (!class_exists('SimpleDB')) require_once('sdb.php');
$sdb = new SimpleDB(awsAccessKey, awsSecretKey);
```

Creating a domain with PHP

A **SimpleDB domain** is a container for storing data, and is similar in concept to a table in a relational database. Once the connection to SimpleDB is made, to create a domain, call the `createDomain` function passing the domain name.

```
$domain = "cars";
$sdb->createDomain($domain);
```

Listing domains with PHP

To display the domains, make a connection, and then call `listDomains`. The function returns an array of values. Retrieving a list of all our domains will return an array of domain names. In addition to the domain name (`$domainname`), the function `domainMetadata` is called to return the information on the domain, such as when the domain was created, the number of items and attributes, and the sizes of attribute names and values.

```
$domainList = $sdb->listDomains();
if ($domainList) {
    foreach ($domainList as $domainName) {
        echo "Domain: <b>$domainName</b><br>";
        print_r($sdb->domainMetadata($domainName));
    }
}
```

Manipulating items with PHP

This sample creates two items in the most basic manner of one at a time. This sample also only deals with a single value for each attribute. Once the connection is made, three variables are prepared. The item name (`$item_name`) is the primary key of the item. An array is built with attribute names and values. Then the three variables are passed to the `putAttributes` function.

```
$domain = "cars";
$item_name = "car1";
$putAttributesRequest["make"] = array("value" => "BMW");
$putAttributesRequest["color"] = array("value" => "grey");
```

```
$putAttributesRequest["year"] = array("value" => "2008");
$putAttributesRequest["desc"] = array("value" => "Sedan");
$putAttributesRequest["model"] = array("value" => "530i");

$sdb->putAttributes($domain,$item_name,$putAttributesRequest);

$item_name = "car2";
$putAttributesRequest["make"] = array("value" => "BMW");
$putAttributesRequest["color"] = array("value" => "white");
$putAttributesRequest["year"] = array("value" => "2007");
$putAttributesRequest["desc"] = array("value" =>
    "Sports Utility Vehicle");
$putAttributesRequest["model"] = array("value" => "X5");

$sdb->putAttributes($domain,$item_name,$putAttributesRequest);
```

You can query for items within a domain by specifying the attribute and value to match. The SELECT syntax is a new addition to SimpleDB and allows searching your domains using simple SQL-like query expressions. The previous version of SimpleDB supported only a query-style syntax that is now being deprecated in favor of the simpler and easier-to-use SELECT expressions. Now that the items are created in the cars domain, we can list them as follows:

```
$domain = "cars";
print_r($sdb->select($domain,"select * from $domain"));
```

To retrieve a select item by the attribute value, you can use the following:

```
$domain = "cars";
$item_make = "BMW";
print_r($sdb->select($domain,"select * from $domain where
                              make='$item_make'"));
```

To retrieve a specific item by the item name, you can use the following:

```
$domain = "cars";
$item_name = "car1";
print_r($sdb->getAttributes($domain,$item_name));
```

To delete a specific item, you can use the following:

```
$domain = "cars";
$item_name = "car1";
$sdb->deleteAttributes($domain,$item_name);
```

To delete specific attribute values, but leave the item, use the following lines of code:

[Note: if all attributes are deleted, then the item is deleted.]

```
$domain = "cars";
$item_name = "car2";
$deleteAttributesRequest = array("make", "color", "year",
    "desc", "model");
$deleteAttributesRequest["desc"] = "Sports Utility Vehicle";
$deleteAttributesRequest["model"] = "X5";
$sdb->deleteAttributes($domain,$item_name,$deleteAttributesRequest);
```

This code deletes the desc and model attributes from the car2 item.

Deleting a domain with PHP

Finally, you delete a domain by specifying its name. Once you delete a domain, the data is gone forever. So use caution when deleting a domain!

```
$domain = "cars";
$sdb->deleteDomain($domain);
```

Basic operations with Python

Prabhakar Chaganti: "My personal preference is for the Python library — boto, which has a very nicely designed interface and a great community of users".

Python is an elegant, open source, object-oriented programming language that is great for rapid application development. Python is a stable, mature language that has been around for quite a long period of time, and is widely used across many of the industries and in a large variety of applications. It comes with an interactive console that can be used for quick evaluation of code snippets and makes experimentation with new APIs very easy. Python is a dynamically-typed language that gives you the power to program in a compact and concise manner. There is no such verbosity that is associated with a statically-typed language such as Java. It will be much easier to grasp the concepts of SimpleDB without drowning in a lot of lines of repetitive code. Most importantly, Python will bring fun back into your programming!

Introducing boto

Boto is an open source Python library for communicating with all of the Amazon web services, including SimpleDB. It was originally conceived by Mitch Garnaat and is currently maintained and enhanced by him and a community of developers. It is by far Prabhakar's favorite library for interacting with AWS, and is very easy to use. Boto works with most recent versions of Python, but please make sure that you are using at least a 2.5.x version of Python. Do not use Python 3.x, as boto will not currently work with it. All versions of Linux usually ship with Python, but if you are running on Windows or Mac OS X, you will need to download and install a version of Python for your platform from `http://python.org/download/`. There are installers available for Windows and Mac OS X, and the installation process is as simple as downloading the correct file and then double-clicking on the file. If you have Python already installed, you can easily verify the version from a terminal window.

```
$ python
```

```
Python 2.5.1 (r251:54863, Feb  6 2009, 19:02:12)
[GCC 4.0.1 (Apple Inc. build 5465)] on darwin
Type "help", "copyright", "credits" or "license" for more information.
>>>
```

You will need a copy of the `setuptools` package before you can install boto. Download the latest version for your platform from the **setuptools** page— `http://pypi.python.org/pypi/setuptools`. If you are on Windows, just run the downloaded EXE file. If you are running on Linux, use your existing package manager to install it. For instance, on Ubuntu, you can install `setuptools` using the apt package manager.

```
$ sudo apt-get install python-setuptools
```

Download boto from the project page at `http://code.google.com/p/boto/`. The latest version at the time of writing this chapter is boto-1.8d, and is provided as a g-zipped distribution that needs to be un-archived after download.

```
$ tar -zxvf boto-1.8d.tar.gz
```

This will create a folder named `boto-1.8d` and un-archive all the files. Now change into this new folder and run the install script to install boto.

```
$ sudo python setup.py install
```

This will byte-compile and install boto into your system. Before you use boto, you must set up your environment so that boto can find your AWS Access key identifiers. You can get your Access Keys from your AWS account page. Set up two environment variables to point to each of the keys.

```
$ export AWS_ACCESS_KEY_ID=Your_AWS_Access_Key_ID
$ export AWS_SECRET_ACCESS_KEY=Your_AWS_Secret_Access_Key
```

You can now check if boto is correctly installed and available by using the Python Interpreter and importing the library. If you don't have any errors, then you have boto installed correctly.

```
$ python
Python 2.5.1 (r251:54863, Feb  6 2009, 19:02:12)
[GCC 4.0.1 (Apple Inc. build 5465)] on darwin
Type "help", "copyright", "credits" or "license" for more information.
>>>
>>> import boto
```

Exploring SimpleDB with Python

We will now use the installed and configured boto library to run some basic operations in SimpleDB using the Python console. This will quickly get you familiar with both boto and various SimpleDB operations. Boto will use the environment variable for the Access Keys that we set up in the previous section for connecting to SimpleDB.

We first create a connection to SimpleDB.

```
>>> import boto
>>> sdb_connection = boto.connect_sdb()
>>>
```

Boto is using the AWS Access Keys we previously set up in the environmental variables in this case. You can also explicitly specify the Access Keys on creation.

```
>>> import boto
>>> sdb_connection = boto.connect_sdb(access_key,secret_key)
>>>
```

Creating a domain with Python

A SimpleDB domain is a container for storing data, and is similar in concept to a table in a relational database. A new domain can be created by specifying a name for the domain.

```
>>> domain1 = sdb_connection.create_domain('prabhakar-dom-1')
>>>
```

Retrieving a domain with Python

Retrieving a list of all our domains will return a Python result set object that can be iterated over in order to access each domain.

```
>>> all_domains = sdb_connection.get_all_domains()
>>>
>>> len(all_domains)
1
>>>
>>> for d in all_domains:
...     print d.name
...
prabhakar-dom-1
```

You can also retrieve a single domain by specifying its name.

```
>>> my_domain = sdb_connection.get_domain('prabhakar-dom-1')
>>>
>>> print my_domain.name
prabhakar-dom-1
```

Creating items with Python

You can create a new item by specifying the attributes for the item along with the name of the item to be created.

```
>>>
>>> my_domain.put_attributes('car1', {'make':'BMW', 'color':'grey','year':'2008','desc':'Sedan','model':'530i'})
>>>
```

```
>>> my_domain.put_attributes('car2', {'make':'BMW', 'color':'white','year
':'2007','desc':' Sports Utility Vehicle','model':'X5'})
>>>
```

Items stored within a domain can be retrieved by specifying the item name. The name of an item must be unique and is similar to the concept of a primary key in a relational database. The uniqueness of the item name within a domain will cause your existing item attributes to be overwritten with the new values if you try to store new attributes with the same item name.

```
>>> my_item = my_domain.get_item('car1')
>>>
>>> print my_item
{u'color': u'grey', u'model': u'530i', u'desc': u'Sedan', u'make':
u'BMW', u'year': u'2008'}
>>>
```

You can query for items within a domain by specifying the attribute and value to match. The SELECT syntax is a new addition to SimpleDB and allows searching your domains using simple SQL-like query expressions. The previous version of SimpleDB only supported a query-style syntax that is now being deprecated in favor of the simpler and easier-to-use SELECT expressions.

```
>>> rs = my_domain.select("SELECT name FROM `prabhakar-dom-1`
    WHERE make='BMW'")
>>> for result in rs:
...     print result.name
...
car1
car2
>>>
```

Multiple attributes can also be specified as a part of the query.

```
>>> rs = my_domain.select("SELECT name FROM `prabhakar-dom-1`
                     WHERE make='BMW' AND model='X5'")
>>> for result in rs:
...     print result.name
...
car2
>>>
```

You can delete a specific item and all of its attributes from a domain.

```
>>> sdb_connection.get_attributes('prabhakar-dom-1','car1')
{u'color': u'grey', u'model': u'530i', u'desc': u'Sedan',
    u'make': u'BMW', u'year': u'2008'}
>>>
>>> sdb_connection.delete_attributes('prabhakar-dom-1','car1')
True
>>> sdb_connection.get_attributes('prabhakar-dom-1',car1')
{}
>>>
```

Finally, you delete a domain by specifying its name. Once you delete a domain, the data is gone forever. So use caution when deleting a domain!

```
>>> sdb_connection.delete_domain('prabhakar-dom-1')
True
>>>
```

Summary

In this chapter, we set up an AWS account, enabled SimpleDB service for the account, and installed and set up libraries for Java, PHP, and Python. We explored several SimpleDB operations using these libraries. In the next chapter, we will examine the differences between SimpleDB and the relational database model in detail.

SimpleDB versus RDBMS

We have all used a **Relational Database Management System (RDBMS)** at some point in our careers. These relational databases are ubiquitous and are available from a wide range of companies such as Oracle, Microsoft, IBM, and so on. These databases have served us well for our application needs. However, there is a new breed of applications coming to the forefront in the current Internet-driven and socially networked economy. The new applications require large scaling to meet demand peaks that can quickly reach massive levels. This is a scenario that is hard to satisfy using a traditional relational database, as it is impossible to requisition and provision the hardware and software resources that will be needed to service the demand peaks. It is also non-trivial and difficult to scale a normal RDBMS to hundreds or thousands of nodes. The overwhelming complexity of doing this makes the RDBMS not viable for these kinds of applications. SimpleDB provides a great alternative to an RDBMS and can provide a solution to all these problems. However, in order to provide this solution, SimpleDB makes some choices and design decisions that you need to understand in order to make an informed choice about the data storage for your application domain.

In this chapter, we are going to discuss the differences between SimpleDB and a traditional RDBMS, as well as the pros and cons of using SimpleDB as the storage engine in your application.

No normalization

Normalization is a process of organizing data efficiently in a relational database by eliminating redundant data, while at the same time ensuring that the data dependencies make sense. SimpleDB data models do not conform to any of the normalization forms, and tend to be completely de-normalized. The lack of need for normalization in SimpleDB allows you a great deal of flexibility with your model, and enables you to use the power of multi-valued attributes in your data.

Let's look at a simple example of a database starting with a basic spreadsheet structure and then design it for an RDBMS and a SimpleDB. In this example, we will create a simple contact database, with contact information as raw data.

ID	First_Name	Last_Name	Phone_Num
101	John	Smith	555-845-7854
101	John	Smith	555-854-9885
101	John	Smith	555-695-7485
102	Bill	Jones	555-748-7854
102	Bill	Jones	555-874-8654

The obvious issue is the repetition of the name data. The table is inefficient and would require care to update to keep the name data in sync. To find a person by his or her phone number is easy.

```
SELECT * FROM Contact_Info WHERE Phone_Num = '555-854-9885'
```

So let's analyze the strengths and weaknesses of this database design.

SCORE—Raw data	Strength	Weakness
Efficient storage		No
Efficient search by phone number	Yes	
Efficient search by name		No
Easy to add another phone number	Yes	

The design is simple, but as the name data is repeated, it would require care to keep the data in sync. Searching for phone numbers by name would be ugly if the names got out of sync.

To improve the design, we can rationalize the data. One approach would be to create multiple phone number fields such as the following. While this is a simple solution, it does limit the phone numbers to three. Add e-mail and Twitter, and the table becomes wider and wider.

ID	First_Name	Last_Name	Phone_Num_1	Phone_Num_2	Phone_Num_3
101	John	Smith	555-845-7854	555-854-9885	555-695-7485
102	Bill	Jones	555-748-7854	555-874-8654	

Finding a person by a phone number is ugly.

```
SELECT * FROM Contact_Info WHERE Phone_Num_1 = '555-854-9885'
OR Phone_Num_2 = '555-854-9885'
OR Phone_Num_3 = '555-854-9885'
```

Now let's analyze the strengths and weaknesses of this database design.

SCORE—Rationalize data	Strength	Weakness
Efficient storage	Yes	
Efficient search by phone number		No
Efficient search by name	Yes	
Easy to add another phone number		No

The design is simple, but the phone numbers are limited to three, and searching by phone number involves three index searches.

Another approach would be to use a delimited list for the phone number as follows:

ID	First_Name	Last_Name	Phone_Nums
101	John	Smith	555-845-7854;555-854-9885;555-695-7485
102	Bill	Jones	555-748-7854;555-874-8654

This approach has the advantage of no data repetition and is easy to maintain, compact, and extendable, but the only way to find a record by the phone number is with a substring search.

```
SELECT * FROM Contact_Info WHERE Phone_Nums LIKE %555-854-9885%
```

This type of SQL forces a complete table scan. Do this with a small table and no one will notice, but try this on a large database with millions of records, and the performance of the database will suffer.

SCORE—Delimited data	Strength	Weakness
Efficient storage	Yes	
Efficient search by phone number		No
Efficient search by name	Yes	
Easy to add another phone number	Yes	

A delimited field is good for data that is of one type and will only be retrieved.

The **normalization** for relational databases results in splitting up your data into separate tables that are related to one another by keys. A **join** is an operation that allows you to retrieve the data back easily across the multiple tables.

Let's first normalize this data.

This is the `Person_Info` table:

ID	First_Name	Last_Name
101	John	Smith
102	Bill	Jones

And this is the `Phone_Info` table:

ID	Phone_Num
101	555-845-7854
101	555-854-9885
101	555-695-7485
102	555-748-7854
102	555-874-8654

Now a join of the `Person_Info` table with the `Phone_Info` can retrieve the list of phone numbers as well as the e-mail addresses. The table structure is clean and other than the ID primary key, no data is duplicated. Provided `Phone_Num` is indexed, retrieving a contact by the phone number is efficient.

```
SELECT First_Name, Last_Name, Phone_num, Person_Info.ID
FROM Person_Info JOIN Phone_Info
ON Person_Info.ID = Phone_Info.ID
WHERE Phone_Num = '555-854-9885'
```

So if we analyze the strengths and weaknesses of this database design, we get:

SCORE—Relational data	Strength	Weakness
Efficient storage	Yes	
Efficient search by phone number	Yes	
Efficient search by name	Yes	
Easy to add another phone number	Yes	

While this is an efficient relational model, there is no `join` command in SimpleDB. Using two tables would force two selects to retrieve the complete contact information. Let's look at how this would be done using the SimpleDB principles.

No joins

SimpleDB does not support the concept of joins. Instead, SimpleDB provides you with the ability to store multiple values for an attribute, thus avoiding the necessity to perform a join to retrieve all the values.

ID			
101	First_Name=John	Last_Name=Smith	Phone_Num = 555-845-7854 Phone_Num = 555-854-9885 Phone_Num = 555-695-7485
102	First_Name=Bill	Last_Name=Jones	Phone_Num = 555-748-7854 Phone_Num = 555-874-8654

In the SimpleDB table, each record is stored as an item with attribute/value pairs. The difference here is that the `Phone_Num` field has multiple values. Unlike a delimited list field, SimpleDB indexes all values enabling an efficient search each value.

```
SELECT * FROM Contact_Info WHERE Phone_Num = '555-854-9885'
```

This `SELECT` is very quick and efficient. It is even possible to use `Phone_Num` multiple times such as follows:

```
SELECT * FROM Contact_Info WHERE Phone_Num = '555-854-9885'
OR Phone_Num = '555-748-7854'
```

Let's analyze the strengths and weaknesses of this approach:

SCORE—SimpleDB data	Strength	Weakness
Efficient storage	Yes	
Efficient search by phone number	Yes	
Efficient search by name	Yes	
Easy to add another phone number	Yes	

No schemas

There are no schemas anywhere in sight of SimpleDB. You don't have to create schemas, change schemas, migrate schemas to a new version, or maintain schemas. This is yet another thing that is difficult for some people from a traditional relational database world to grasp, but this flexibility is one of the keys to the power of scaling offered by SimpleDB. You can store any attribute-value data you like in any way you want. If the requirements for your application should suddenly change and you need to start storing data on a customer's Twitter handle for instance, all you need to do is store the data without worrying about any schema changes!

Let's add an e-mail address to the database in the previous example. In the relational database, it is necessary to either add e-mail to the phone table with a type of contact field or add another field. Let's add another table named `Email_Info`.

`Person_Info` table:

ID	First_Name	Last_Name
101	John	Smith
102	Bill	Jones

`Phone_Info` table:

ID	Phone_Num
101	555-845-7854
101	555-854-9885
101	555-695-7485
102	555-748-7854
102	555-874-8654

`Email_Info` table:

ID	Email_Addr
101	john@abc.ccc
102	bill@def.ccc

Using a traditional relational database approach, we join the three tables to extract the requested data in one call.

```
SELECT First_Name, Last_Name, Phone_num, Person_Info.ID, Email_Addr
FROM Person_Info JOIN Phone_Info JOIN Email_Info
ON Person_Info.ID = Phone_Info.ID
AND Person_Info.ID = Email_Info.ID
WHERE Phone_Num = '555-854-9885'
```

Now let's analyze the strengths and weaknesses of this approach:

SCORE — Relational data	Strength	Weakness
Efficient storage	Yes	
Efficient search by phone number, email	Yes	
Efficient search by name	Yes	
Easy to add another phone number	Yes	
Expandable	Yes	New table defined Two joins required

We ignored the issue of join versus **left outer join**, which is really what should be used here unless all contacts have a phone number and e-mail address. The example is just to illustrate that the Contact_Info schema must be modified.

Contact_Info domain:

ID			
101	First_Name = John	Last_Name = Smith	Phone_Num = 555-845-7854 Phone_Num = 555-854-9885 Phone_Num = 555-695-7485
			Email_Addr = john@abc.ccc
102	First_Name = Bill	Last_Name = Jones	Phone_Num = 555-748-7854 Phone_Num = 555-874-8654
			Email_Addr = john@def.ccc

The obvious question is why is `Email_Addr` not in its own column? In SimpleDB, there is no concept of a column in a table. The spreadsheet view of the SimpleDB data was done for ease of readability, not because it reflects the data structure. The only structure in SimpleDB consists of the item name and attribute/value pairs. The proper representation of the SimpleDB data is:

ID	Attribute/Value pairs
101	First_Name = John Last_Name = Smith Phone_Num = 555-845-7854 Phone_Num = 555-854-9885 Phone_Num = 555-695-7485 Email_Addr = john@abc.ccc
102	First_Name = Bill Last_Name = Jones Phone_Num = 555-748-7854 Phone_Num = 555-874-8654 Email_Addr = john@def.ccc

Use the following query to fetch a contact item by the e-mail address:

```
SELECT * FROM Contact_Info WHERE Email_Addr = 'john@def.ccc'
```

Let's analyze the strengths and weaknesses of this approach:

SCORE—SimpleDB data	Strength	Weakness
Efficient storage	Yes	
Efficient search by phone number, email	Yes	
Efficient search by name	Yes	
Easy to add another phone number	Yes	
Expandable	Yes	

Simpler SQL

Structured Query Language (SQL) is a standard language that is widely used for accessing and manipulating the data stored in a relational database. SQL has evolved over the years into a highly complex language that can do a vast variety of things to your database. SimpleDB does not support the complete SQL language, but instead it lets you perform your data retrieval using a much smaller and simpler subset of an SQL-like query language. This simplifies the whole process of querying your data. A big difference between the simpler SQL supported by SimpleDB and SQL is the support for multi-valued SimpleDB attributes, which makes it super simple to query your data and get back multiple values for an attribute.

The syntax of the SimpleDB SQL is summarized in this syntax:

```
select output_list
from domain_name
[where expression]
[sort_instructions]
[limit limit]
```

We will go into detail on SimpleDB SQL in *Chapter 6, Querying*.

Only strings

SimpleDB uses a very simple data model, and all data is stored as an UTF-8 string. This simplified textual data makes it easy for SimpleDB to automatically index your data and give you the ability to retrieve the data very quickly. If you need to store and retrieve other kinds of data types such as numbers and dates, you must encode these data types into strings whose lexicographical ordering will be the same as your intended ordering of the data. As SimpleDB does not have the concept of schemas that enforce type correctness for your domains, it is the developer's responsibility to ensure the correct encoding of data before storage into SimpleDB.

Working only in strings impacts two aspects of using the database: queries and sorts.

Consider the following `Sample_Qty` table:

ID	
101	Quantity = 1.0
102	Quantity = 1.00
103	Quantity = 10
104	Quantity = 25
105	Quantity = 100

Now try and execute the following SQL statement:

```
SELECT * FROM Sample_Qty WHERE Quantity= '1'
```

This SQL statement will retrieve nothing—not even items 101 and 102.

Selecting all records sorted by Quantity will return the order 101, 102, 103, 105, 104.

Dates present an easier problem, as they can be stored in ISO 8601 format to enable sorting as well as predictable searching. We will cover this in detail in *Chapter 5, Data Types*.

Eventual consistency

Simple DB can be thought of as a Write-Seldom-Read-Many model. Updates are done to a central database, but reads can be done from many read-only database slave servers.

SimpleDB keeps multiple copies of each domain. Whenever data is written or updated within a domain, first a success status code is returned to your application, and then all the different copies of the data are updated. The propagation of these changes to all of the nodes at all the storage locations might take some time, but eventually the data will become consistent across all the nodes.

SimpleDB provides this assurance only of eventual consistency for your data. This means that the data you retrieve from SimpleDB at any particular time may be slightly out of date. The main reason for this is that SimpleDB service is implemented as a distributed system, and all of the information is stored across multiple physical servers and potentially across multiple data centers in a completely redundant manner. This ensures the large-scale ready accessibility and safety of your data, but comes at the cost of a slight delay before any addition, alteration, or deletion operations you perform on the data being propagated throughout the entire distributed SimpleDB system. Your data will eventually be globally consistent, but until it is consistent, the possibility of retrieving slightly outdated information from SimpleDB exists.

Amazon has stated in the past that states of global consistency across all the nodes will usually be achieved "within seconds"; however, please be aware that this timeframe will depend to a great degree on the processing and the network load on SimpleDB at the time that you make a change to your data. An intermediate caching layer can quickly solve this consistency issue if data consistency is highly important and essential to your application. The principle of eventual consistency is the hardest to grasp, and it is the biggest difference between a RDBMS and SimpleDB. In order to scale massively, this is a trade-off that needs to be made at design time for your application. If you consider how often you will require immediate consistency within your web applications, you might find that this trade-off is well worth the improved scalability of your application.

Flash: February 24, 2010 — consistent read added

While eventual consistency is still the normal mode for SimpleDB, Amazon announced several extensions for consistent read. When using a `GetAttributes` or `SELECT`, the `ConsistentRead = true` can be selected, forcing a read of the most current value. This tells SimpleDB to read the items from the master database rather than from one of the slaves, guaranteeing the latest updates or deletes. This does not mean you can use this on all reads and still get the extreme scaling. In *Chapter 8, Tuning and Usage Costs*, we will look at the cost of using consistent reads.

A conditional PUT or DELETE was also announced, which will execute a database PUT or DELETE only if the consistent read of a specific attribute has a specific value or does not exist. This is useful if concurrent controls or counters primitives. In later chapters, we will look at the implications of these new features.

Scalability

Relational databases are designed around the entities and the relationships between the entities, and need a large investment in hardware and servers in order to provide high scaling. SimpleDB provides a great alternative that is designed around partitioning your data into independent chunks that are stored in a distributed manner and can scale up massively. SimpleDB provides the automatic partitioning and replication of your data, while at the same time guaranteeing fast access and reliability for your data. You can let Amazon scale their platform as needed using their extensive resources, while you enjoy the ability to easily scale up in response to increased demand!

The best feature of SimpleDB scalability is that you only pay for usage, not for the large cluster needed in anticipation of large usage.

Low maintenance

Maintaining a relational database and keeping it humming with indexing takes effort, know-how, and technical and administrative resources. Applications are not static but dynamic things, and change constantly along with additions of new features. All of these updates can result in changes and modifications to the database schema along with increased maintenance and tuning costs. SimpleDB is hosted and maintained for you by Amazon. Your task is as simple as storing your data and retrieving it when needed. The simplicity of structured data and lack of schemas helps your application be more flexible and adaptable to change, which is always around the corner. SimpleDB ensures that your queries are optimized and retrieval times are fast by indexing all your data automatically.

Advantages of the SimpleDB model

SimpleDB's alternative approach for storing data can be advantageous for meeting your application needs when compared to a traditional relational database. Here's the list of advantages:

- Reduced maintenance as compared to a relational database
- Automated indexing of your data for fast performance
- Flexibility to modify or change your stored data without the need to worry about schemas
- Failover for your data automatically being provided by Amazon
- Replication for your data across multiple nodes also handled for you by Amazon
- Ability to easily scale up in response to increased demand without worrying about running out of hardware or processing capacity
- Simplified data storage and querying using a simple API
- The lack of object-to-relational mapping that is common for an RDBMS allows your structured data to map more directly to your underlying application code and reduce the application development time

Disadvantages of the SimpleDB model

SimpleDB's alternative approach also has some disadvantages compared to a relational database for certain applications.

- Those using applications that always need to ensure immediate consistency of data will find that SimpleDB's eventual data consistency model may not suit their needs. The consistent read announcement does change this, but the eventual consistency model is still the basis of the extreme scalability.

- Using SimpleDB as the data storage engine in your applications needs the development team to get used to different concepts over a simple, traditional RDBMS.

- Because relationships are not explicitly defined at the schema level as in a relational database, you might need to enforce some data constraints within your application code.

- If your application needs to store data other than strings, such as numbers and dates, additional effort will be required on your part to encode the strings before storing them in the SimpleDB format.

- The ability to have multiple attributes for an item is a completely different way of storing data and has a learning curve attached to it for new users who are exposed to SimpleDB.

Summary

In this chapter, we discussed the differences between SimpleDB and the traditional relational database systems in detail. In the next chapter, we are going to review the data model used by SimpleDB.

4

The SimpleDB Data Model

The entire data model for SimpleDB is comprised of four concepts—domains, items, attributes, and values. We will explore these concepts in detail in this chapter. The conceptual hierarchy of a domain in SimpleDB is like the following chart and shows the relation between the different components.

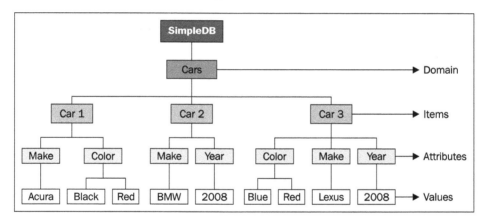

In this chapter, we will cover:

- Interacting with a domain
- Metadata for a domain
- Interacting with items in a domain
- Interacting with the attributes of an item
- Storing multiple values for an attribute
- SimpleDB constraints on domain, items, attributes, and attribute values
- Consistent Read and Conditional Put/Delete announced on February 24, 2010

Domains

A **domain** is a container that lets you store your structured data and run queries against it. The data is stored in the domain as **items**. A domain is similar to a worksheet tab in a spreadsheet, while items are similar in concept to the rows in the spreadsheet. You can run queries against a domain, but you cannot yet query across domains in the current version of SimpleDB. Each domain in your SimpleDB account is completely distinct from all your other domains, and therefore the items stored in one domain are completely separate from the items stored in other domains. This is why queries cannot be performed across domains. You can place all of your data in a single domain or partition it across multiple domains, depending on the nature of the data and the application. You can create a domain called *cars* and use it or you can partition the data into separate domains such as brands beginning with A-J in CARSAJ, beginning with K-T in CARSKT, and so on. SimpleDB gives you the freedom to partition the data however you like.

Domains with Java

You can create a domain using the `SimpleDB` class in Typica.

```
SimpleDB sdb = new SimpleDB(awsAccessId, awsSecretKey, true);
try {
    Domain domain = sdb.createDomain("Cars");
    System.out.println(domain.getName());
} catch (SDBException ex) {
    System.out.println(ex.getMessage());
}
```

Typica provides several methods for interacting with a domain and performing various operations on it.

- `batchPutAttributes`: This method is used to batch-insert multiple items without attributes.
- `deleteItem`: This method is used to delete an item.
- `getItem`: This method is used to get an item object without getting a list of them.
- `getItemsAttributes`: This method is used to get attributes of given items.
- `getMetadata`: This method is used to returns information about the domain.
- `getName`: This method is used to get the name of the domain represented by this object.
- `listItems`: This method is used to get a list of all items in this domain.

- `listItemsAttributes`: This method is used to get attributes of items specified in the query string.

- `listItemsWithAttributes`: This method is used to get a list of items (with attributes) in this domain filtered by the query string.

Domains with PHP

You can create a domain in PHP with the following:

```
$sdb = new SimpleDB(awsAccessKey, awsSecretKey);
$sdb->createDomain("Cars");
```

Our sample PHP library provides a number of functions for accessing SimpleDB:

- `deleteDomain`: This method is used to delete a domain.

- `listDomains`: This method is used to list all domains.

- `domainMetadata`: This method is used to return information about a specific domain.

- `select`: This method is used to get the attributes/values for an SQL query.

- `getAttributes`: This method is used to get the attributes/values for a specific item.

- `putAttributes`: This method is used to put the attributes/values for a specific item.

- `batchPutAttributes`: This method is used to batch-put attributes/values for a group of items.

- `deleteAttributes`: This method is used to delete attributes/values for a specific item.

 The SDB-PHP API supports the newly-added capabilities of Consistent Read and Conditional Put/Delete from February 24, 2010.

Domains with Python

Here is how you would create the same `Cars` domain using **boto**:

```
>>>cars_domain = sdb_connection.create_domain('Cars')
Domain:Cars
>>>
```

The domain object created here provides all of the methods that we need for interacting with the Cars domain.

You can use the inspect module to list all of the boto methods for interacting with a domain.

```
>>>importinspect
>>>
>>> import pprint
>>> pp = pprint.PrettyPrinter(indent=4)
>>>
>>> pp.pprint(inspect.getmembers(cars_domain, inspect.ismethod))
[    ('__init__', <bound method Domain.__init__ of Domain:Cars>),
     ('__iter__', <bound method Domain.__iter__ of Domain:Cars>),
     ('__repr__', <bound method Domain.__repr__ of Domain:Cars>),
     (    'batch_put_attributes',
<bound method Domain.batch_put_attributes of Domain:Cars>),
     (    'delete_attributes',
<bound method Domain.delete_attributes of Domain:Cars>),
     ('delete_item', <bound method Domain.delete_item of Domain:Cars>),
     ('endElement', <bound method Domain.endElement of Domain:Cars>),
     ('from_xml', <bound method Domain.from_xml of Domain:Cars>),
     ('get_attributes', <bound method Domain.get_attributes of
Domain:Cars>),
     ('get_item', <bound method Domain.get_item of Domain:Cars>),
      ('get_metadata', <bound method Domain.get_metadata of Domain:Cars>),
     ('new_item', <bound method Domain.new_item of Domain:Cars>),
     ('put_attributes', <bound method Domain.put_attributes of
Domain:Cars>),
     ('query', <bound method Domain.query of Domain:Cars>),
     ('select', <bound method Domain.select of Domain:Cars>),
     ('startElement', <bound method Domain.startElement of Domain:Cars>),
     ('to_xml', <bound method Domain.to_xml of Domain:Cars>)]
>>>
```

The methods provided by **boto** for interacting with a domain are as follows:

- `batch_put_attributes`: This method is used to store attributes for multiple items with a single call. This is a nice way to batch things together to avoid the overhead of making multiple calls to SimpleDB, each of which stores attributes for a single item.

- `delete_attributes`: This method is used to delete the attributes from a given item.

- `delete_item`: This method is used to delete the specified item from the domain.

- `get_attributes`: This method is used to retrieve the attributes for a given item. You can either get all the attributes for an item, or specify the names of attributes of interest.

- `get_item`: This method is used to retrieve the specified item and all its attributes from the domain.

- `put_attributes`: This method is used to store attributes for a given item.

- `query`: This method is used to return a list of items within domain that match the query.

- `select`: This method is used to return a set of attributes for item names within the domain that match the query expression. The query must be expressed in using the recently-introduced SELECT-style syntax rather than the original SimpleDB query language.

Exploring the metadata for a domain and costs

Every call made to SimpleDB, irrespective of whether the operation works on a domain or an item, always returns two specific values associated with it. These values are automatically provided within the response. They exist for all operations, and for every invocation of the operation in SimpleDB:

- `RequestId`: A unique ID for tracking the request made to SimpleDB. This is also very useful for debugging purposes. If you are having any issues with your calls to SimpleDB and are unable to determine the cause or reason from your side, this is the ID that you need to give AWS as a part of the debug information to facilitate tracing the request.

- `BoxUsage`: SimpleDB measures the machine utilization of each request and charges the customer based on the amount of machine capacity used to complete the particular request (SELECT, GET, PUT, and so on), normalized to the hourly capacity of a circa 2007 1.7 GHz Xeon processor. This measure is named as **BoxUsage** and its value is returned as part of the response for every call made to SimpleDB. BoxUsage is a number that you can use for tuning your queries based on the fact that the longer a query takes to run, the higher its BoxUsage value.

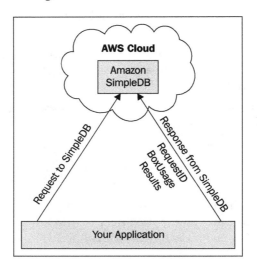

Colin Percival has a great dissection of the BoxUsage values returned by SimpleDB on his blog (http://www.daemonology.net/blog/2008-06-25-dissecting-simpledb-boxusage.html) and provides this breakdown of the costs associated with the calls made to SimpleDB.

Request type	BoxUsage (hours)	BoxUsage (seconds)	Overhead cost (µ$)	Variable cost (µ$)
CreateDomain DeleteDomain	0.0055590278	4803 / 240	778.264	
ListDomains	0.0000071759	(6 + 1/5) / 240	1.005	
PutAttributes (N attributes specified) DeleteAttributes (N attributes specified)	$0.0000219907 + 0.0000000002\ N^3$	$19 / 240 + 0.00000072\ N^3$	3.079	$0.000028\ N^3$
GetAttributes (N values returned)	$0.0000093202 + 0.0000000020\ N^2$	$(8 + 1/19) / 240 + 0.00000720\ N^2$	1.305	$0.000280\ N^2$

Request type	BoxUsage (hours)	BoxUsage (seconds)	Overhead cost (µ$)	Variable cost (µ$)
Query (N items returned)	0.0000140000 + 0.0000000080 N or more	0.0504 + 0.00002880 N or more	1.960	0.001120 N or more

 These numbers and the associated costs for each type of SimpleDB are interesting, but please keep in mind that these costs will change as AWS adjusts the service and changes the pricing.

The costs incurred by you when using SimpleDB also include the cost for storing the actual data, which is separate from the BoxUsage values.

Retrieving domain metadata

You can also retrieve system statistics about the data contained within a specified domain. These statistics provide some very useful metadata that can give you a good idea about how you are using SimpleDB.

Retrieving domain metadata with Java

Typica provides a method named `getMetadata()` on a domain object that can be used for retrieving the metadata information. You can retrieve the values for the `requestID` and `boxusage` for every call that is made to SimpleDB.

```
SimpleDB sdb = new SimpleDB(awsAccessId, awsSecretKey, true);
try {
    Domain domain = sdb.getDomain("songs");
    DomainMetadataResult metadata = domain.getMetadata();
    System.out.println(" ItemCount: " + metadata.getItemCount());
    System.out.println(" AttributeNameCount: "
                        + metadata.getAttributeNameCount());
    System.out.println(" AttributeValueCount: "
                        + metadata.getAttributeValueCount());
    System.out.println(" ItemNamesSizeBytes: "
                        + metadata.getItemNamesSizeBytes());
    System.out.println(" AttributeNamesSizeBytes: "
                        + metadata.getAttributeNamesSizeBytes());
    System.out.println(" AttributeValuesSizeBytes: "
                        + metadata.getAttributeValuesSizeBytes());
    System.out.println(" Timestamp: " + metadata.getTimestamp());
```

```
      System.out.println(" BoxUsage: " + metadata.getBoxUsage());
      System.out.println(" RequestID: " + metadata.getRequestId());
} catch (SDBException ex) {
      System.out.println(ex.getMessage());
}
```

Retrieving domain metadata with PHP

The `domainMetadata` function returns an array of values for an existing domain.
If the domain does not exist; an error is returned.

```php
$sdb = new SimpleDB(awsAccessKey, awsSecretKey);
  // create connection
$domain = "car-s";
$rest = $sdb->domainMetadata($domainName);
  // returns an array with names
echo("ItemCount: ".$rest["ItemCount"]."\n");
echo("ItemNamesSizeBytes: ".$rest["ItemNamesSizeBytes"]."\n");
echo("AttributeNameCount: ".$rest["AttributeNameCount"]."\n");
echo("AttributeNamesSizeBytes: "
    .$rest["AttributeNamesSizeBytes"]."\n");
echo("AttributeValueCount: ".$rest["AttributeValueCount"]."\n");
echo("AttributeValuesSizeBytes: "
    .$rest["AttributeValuesSizeBytes"]."\n");
echo("Timestamp: ".$rest["Timestamp"]." "
    . date("M j,Y g:iA",$rest["Timestamp"]) . "\n");
echo("RequestId: ".$sdb->RequestId."\n");
echo("BoxUsage: ".$sdb->BoxUsage." = "
    . SimpleDB::displayUsage($sdb->BoxUsage)."<br>");
```

Accessing the values is a simple array reference. Using the domain metadata call
is a low-cost way to validate that a specific domain exists.

Retrieving domain metadata with Python

Boto provides the box usage and request ID values for each call that we make to
SimpleDB, as attributes on the object that is returned as a result of the call. In case of
the domain that we created above, for instance, we can easily get these values from
the `cars_domain` object.

```
>>>
>>> cars_domain.BoxUsage
u'0.0000091640'
>>>
>>> cars_domain.RequestId
```

```
u'6d7a96bd-6ac5-828c-9a48-ec5fa1920803'
>>>
>>>
>>>
>>> cars_metadata = cars_domain.get_metadata()
>>>
>>> cars_metadata.attr_name_count
0
>>>
>>> cars_metadata.attr_names_size
0
>>>
>>> cars_metadata.attr_value_count
0
>>>
>>> cars_metadata.attr_values_size
0
>>>
>>> cars_metadata.item_count
0
>>>
>>> cars_metadata.item_names_size
0
>>>
>>> cars_metadata.timestamp
u'1254073990'
>>>
>>> cars_metadata.BoxUsage
u'0.0000071759'
>>>
>>> cars_metadata.RequestId
u'65fa544a-036b-b897-2fd7-cb50a4b5cfc2'
>>>
```

Components of a domain's metadata

The metadata associated with each domain is:

- Date and time the metadata was last updated.
- Number of all items in the domain. The SELECT API now includes a `count` keyword that can be used for getting much more useful item counts than this specific metadata.
- Number of all attribute's name/value pairs in the domain.
- Number of unique attribute names in the domain.
- Total size of all item names in the domain, in bytes.
- Total size of all attribute values, in bytes.
- Total size of all unique attribute names, in bytes.

The following figure displays visually the various components that comprise the metadata for a SimpleDB domain:

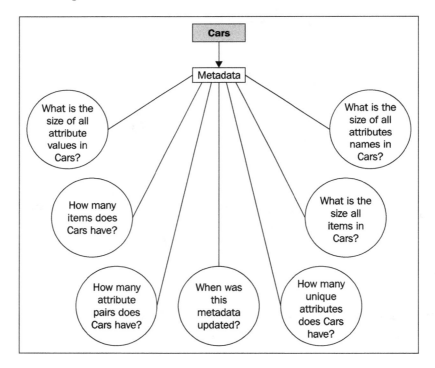

SimpleDB domain constraints

You should also be familiar with some of the constraints and limitations when using the SimpleDB domains.

- **Number of domains**: Each SimpleDB account is by default allowed to create up to 100 domains. If your architecture or system design should need more than 100 domains, you can request AWS to increase the limit. Normally it takes about two business days for the request to be approved. You need to fill out a form on the SimpleDB site (`http://aws.amazon.com/contact-us/simpledb-limit-request/`) to submit your request.

- **Size of domain**: The size of a single domain is limited to 10 GB of data. This includes all the storage used by the data for the domain. This is a hard limit and currently there is no way to request for an increase.

- **Number of attributes**: The total number of attributes stored in a domain is limited to one billion per domain. That is a lot of attributes, and most applications should comfortably fit within this limit. This is considered per domain, so with the default number of 100 domains, you are looking at a total allowed limit of 100 billion attributes! Partitioning data across multiple domains can be used to get around the limit.

- **Name of a domain**: The name of a domain must be at least three characters in length and a maximum of 255 characters. The allowed characters in the name are a-z, A-Z, 0-9, _, ., and -.

Items

Items represent individual objects within each domain, and each item contains attributes with values. Each item is conceptually similar to a row in a spreadsheet. Items are distinguished by the presence of a unique ID, which can also be used when querying for a specific item.

 This unique identifier is not automatically provided by SimpleDB, and is the responsibility of the developer.

A common scheme followed by users of SimpleDB is to generate **Globally Unique Identifiers** or **GUIDs** and use them as the key for each item. You are not required to use this scheme and are free to generate this ID anyway you like as long as it is unique. The ID also needs to be unique only within the domain of interest.

The February 24, 2010 announcement added capabilities that aid in doing a counter GUID. The Consistent Read and Conditional Put/Delete capabilities are documented at the end of this chapter.

You can add attributes to an item in SimpleDB. Any items that you create that do not have any attributes will not be returned in queries.

 SimpleDB treats empty items as non-existent.

Adding attributes to an item with Java

You must create a list of attributes and then add those attributes to an item in your domain when using Typica.

```java
SimpleDB sdb = new SimpleDB(awsAccessId, awsSecretKey, true);
try {
    Domain domain = sdb.getDomain("Cars");
    Item item = domain.getItem("Car 1");
    List<ItemAttribute> list = new ArrayList<ItemAttribute>();
    list.add(new ItemAttribute("make", "BMW", false));
    list.add(new ItemAttribute("color", "Black", false));
    item.putAttributes(list);

    Item saved_item = domain.getItem("Car 1");
    for (ItemAttribute attr : saved_item.getAttributes()) {
        System.out.println("  " + attr.getName() + " = " + attr
            .getValue());
    }
    item = domain.getItem("Car 1");
    list = new ArrayList<ItemAttribute>();
    list.add(new ItemAttribute("make", "BMW", true));
    list.add(new ItemAttribute("color", "Blue", true));
    item.putAttributes(list);

    Item updated_item = domain.getItem("Car 1");
    for (ItemAttribute attr : updated_item.getAttributes()) {
        System.out.println("  " + attr.getName() + " = " + attr
            .getValue());
    }
    domain.deleteItem("Car 1");
} catch (SDBException ex) {
    System.out.println(ex.getMessage());
}
```

Adding attributes to an item with PHP

You can use the `putAttributes` method on an SDB connection object to add an item, and specify the domain, a unique name for the item, and the list of attributes for the item.

```php
$sdb = new SimpleDB(awsAccessKey, awsSecretKey);
  // create connection

$domain = "car-s";

$item_name = "car1";
echo "putAttributes() record 1<br>";
$putAttributesRequest["make"] = array("value" => "Acura");
  // Example add an attribute
$putAttributesRequest["color"] =
    array("value" => array("Black","Red"));
  // Add multiple values
$rest = $sdb->
    putAttributes($domain,$item_name,$putAttributesRequest);
if ($rest) {
    echo("Record $item_name created");
    echo("RequestId: ".$sdb->RequestId."<br>");
    echo("BoxUsage: ".$sdb->BoxUsage." = "
        . SimpleDB::displayUsage($sdb->BoxUsage)."<br>");
} else {
    echo("Record $item_name FAILED<br>");
    echo("ErrorCode: ".$sdb->ErrorCode."<p>");
}
```

In this example, item `car1` is put into domain `car-s`. Two attributes are added to item `car1`: attribute `make` with value `Acura` and attribute `color` with two values `Black` and `Red`.

Adding attributes to an item with Python

You can use the `put_attributes` method on an SDB connection object to add an item, and specify the domain, a unique name for the item, and the list of attributes for the item.

```python
>>>
>>> item1 = sdb_connection.put_attributes('Cars','Car 1', {})
>>> cars_domain.get_item('Car 1')
>>>
```

You can also use the `put_attributes()` method that is available on a domain object to add a new item in exactly the same way.

```
>>> item2 = cars_domain.put_attributes('Car 2',{'make':'BMW',
'color':'Black'})
>>>
>>> cars_domain.get_item('Car 2')
{u'color': u'Black', u'make': u'BMW'}
>>>
```

The query for the item `Car 2` returned the item as the item was not empty and already had attributes. Now we will add attributes to the empty item and then watch it show up again when we try to get the item from the domain! You can replace the attributes for an item by specifying a true value for the replace parameter in the `put_attributes()` method.

```
>>> item1 = cars_domain.put_attributes('Car 1',{'make':'BMW',
'color':'Black'},True)
>>> cars_domain.get_item('Car 1')
{u'color': u'Black', u'make': u'BMW'}
>>>
```

The methods and fields provided by **boto** on an item object for interacting with the item are:

- `add_value`: This method will add a new attribute key and value to the item. It makes sure you call `save()` to actually persist your additions to SimpleDB.
- `get`: This method will retrieve the value of the specified attribute for the item.
- `delete`: This method will delete all the attributes for the item.
- `has_key`: This method will check if the item has the specified attribute.
- `iterkeys`: This method will retrieve an iterator that will let you iterate through the attributes keys for the item.
- `itervalues`: This method will retrieve an iterator that will let you iterate through the attributes values for the item.
- `keys`: This method will return a list of all the attribute keys for the item.
- `values`: This method will return a list of all the attribute values for the item.
- `load`: This method will reload the item's state from SimpleDB. Be careful when using this method. If you make changes to your item locally, but do not persist those changes to SimpleDB by calling `save()`, then this method will overwrite those changes on your object by refreshing it with the data from SimpleDB.

- update: This method will update the item by providing a Python dictionary with the attribute key/value pairs. You must once again call `save()` in order to persist the changes.

- save: This method will save the changes made to the item to SimpleDB by replacing the item in SimpleDB.

You can do all of these operations using boto as shown below:

```
>>> myitem1 = cars_domain.get_item('Car 1')
>>>
>>> myitem1.add_value('Model','530i')
>>>
>>> myitem1.save()
>>>
>>> myitem1.get('Model')
'530i'
>>>
>>> myitem1.has_key('Model')
True
>>>
>>> for i in myitem1.iterkeys():
...     print i
...
color
make
Model
>>>
>>> for i in myitem1.itervalues():
...     print i
...
Black
BMW
530i
>>>
>>> myitem1.keys()
[u'color', u'make', 'Model']
>>>
```

```
>>> myitem1.update({'Model':'X5'})
>>> myitem1.save()
>>>
>>> myitem1.values()
[u'Black', u'X5', u'BMW']
>>>
>>> myitem1.delete()
>>>
>>> myitem1.load()
>>>
>>> myitem1.values()
[]
>>>
```

Constraints on SimpleDB items

The constraints that you need to be aware of when working with SimpleDB items are:

- The length of the name for an item cannot be more than 1024 bytes.
- Each item can have a maximum 256 name/value pairs per item in a domain.
- The name of an item must only use characters that are UTF-8 characters, which are valid in XML documents. Control characters and any sequences that are not valid in XML are not allowed for use as part of an item name.

Attributes

Each item will have attributes, which are similar in concept to a column in a spreadsheet or a column in a database table. Each attribute is a key/value pair. The key is the unique name for the attribute and the value is the textual data for that key. SimpleDB is schemaless and allows you to have different attributes for each item in a domain. This is impossible in a relational database world where you must define your table schemas up front, and every time you need to add a new field or column, you must upgrade the schema for the database, or your existing applications might start throwing errors. SimpleDB frees you from this upgrade and maintenance cycle, and gives you the freedom to use this flexibility to your advantage when designing your applications.

If you add a new attribute to an item in a domain, only that item will have that attribute, and all the other existing items in the domain will hum along nicely without that additional attribute! You can see this in the following code samples.

Attributes with Java

Typica makes it really easy to add and manipulate the attributes of an item. The general pattern is to create a list of attributes and use the list to specify an item's attributes.

```java
SimpleDB sdb = new SimpleDB(awsAccessId, awsSecretKey, true);
try {
    Domain domain = sdb.getDomain("Cars");
    Item item = domain.getItem("Car 1");
    List<ItemAttribute> list = new ArrayList<ItemAttribute>();
    list.add(new ItemAttribute("make", "Mercedes", false));
    list.add(new ItemAttribute("color", "White", false));
    item.putAttributes(list);

    Item saved_item = domain.getItem("Car 1");
    for (ItemAttribute attr : saved_item.getAttributes()) {
        System.out.println("  " + attr.getName() + " = " + attr
            .getValue());
    }

    item = domain.getItem("Car 2");
    list = new ArrayList<ItemAttribute>();
    list.add(new ItemAttribute("make", "BMW", true));
    list.add(new ItemAttribute("color", "Black", true));
    item.putAttributes(list);

    saved_item = domain.getItem("Car 2");
    for (ItemAttribute attr : saved_item.getAttributes()) {
        System.out.println("  " + attr.getName() + " = " + attr
            .getValue());
    }

    item = domain.getItem("Car 1");
    list = new ArrayList<ItemAttribute>();
    list.add(new ItemAttribute("year", "2009", true));
    item.putAttributes(list);

    item = domain.getItem("Car 1");
    for (ItemAttribute attr : saved_item.getAttributes()) {
        System.out.println("  " + attr.getName() + " = " + attr
            .getValue());
    }
```

```
} catch (SDBException ex) {
    System.out.println(ex.getMessage());
}
```

Attributes with PHP

Consider the following PHP code sample:

```php
$sdb = new SimpleDB(awsAccessKey, awsSecretKey); // create connection

$item_name = "car1";

// Add an attribute
$putAttributesRequest["make"] = array("value" => "BMW");

$putAttributesRequest["color"] = array("value" => "red");

$putAttributesRequest["year"] = array("value" => "2008");

// Replace existing values
$putAttributesRequest["desc"] = array("value" => "Sedan",
                                        "replace" => "true");

$putAttributesRequest["model"] = array("value" => "530i");

$sdb->putAttributes($domain,$item_name,$putAttributesRequest);
```

There are two examples of adding an attribute in this example. In the first example, we are adding a make of "BMW." In the second one, we are replacing a desc of "Sedan."

1. `$putAttributesRequest["make"] = array("value" => "BMW");`

   This line adds a single attribute/value pair.

   In this example, BMW will set as the value for make in item car1. Let's look at several possible situations.

Before	After (replace not specified)
No Make	Make = BMW for item car1
Make = BMW for item car1	Make = BMW for item car1 (no change)
Make = Mercedes for item car1	Make = Mercedes and Make = BMW for item car1

2. `$putAttributesRequest["desc"] = array("value" => "Sedan", "replace" => "true");`

   The addition of the replace parameter set to true forces the current value(s) to be replaced with this value(s).

Before	After (replace=true)
No desc	desc=Sedan for item car1
desc=Sedan for item car1	desc=Sedan for item car1 (no change)
desc=SUV for item car1	desc=Sedan for item car1

Attributes with Python

Python code is a little more succinct, but follows a similar pattern for adding and modifying an item's attributes.

```
 >>> cars __domain.get_item('Car 1')
{u'color': u'White', u'make': u'Mercedes'}
>>>
>>> cars_domain.get_item('Car 2')
{u'color': u'Black', u'make': u'BMW'}
>>>
>>> myitem1 = cars_domain.get_item('Car 1')
>>> myitem1.add_value('year','2009')
>>> myitem1.save()
>>> myitem1
{u'color': u'White', u'make': u'Mercedes', 'year': '2009'}
>>> myitem2
{u'color': u'Black', u'make': u'BMW'}
>>>
```

Constraints on SimpleDB item attributes

Simple DB item attributes have the following constraints:

- The length of the name for an attribute cannot be more than 1024 bytes.

- The name of an attribute must only use characters that are UTF-8 characters, which are valid in XML documents. Control characters and any sequences that are not valid in XML are not allowed for use as part of an attribute name.

Values

Each attribute is a key/value pair, and the value is where you store the interesting stuff—your data! You can only store textual data in SimpleDB for now. There are some ways to get around it and store binary data in Amazon S3 and use metadata in SimpleDB to point to it. We will discuss the procedures for accomplishing this in *Chapter 7, Storing Data on S3*. The only restriction textual data has, with a larger implication, is that you must encode and decode values for other data types such as dates and numbers when storing and retrieving them for use in your application. In the next chapter, we will review how to encode and decode data correctly so that we can do sorting and comparison correctly even for data types such as numbers and dates.

One of the unique features of SimpleDB is the ability to have multiple values for a single attribute. These multiple values are actually stored by SimpleDB in such a way that you can query for each separately!

Storing multiple values in a single attribute with Java

You can store multiple values for an item by specifying the attribute multiple times with different values.

```java
SimpleDB sdb = new SimpleDB(awsAccessId, awsSecretKey, true);
try {
    Domain domain = sdb.getDomain("Cars");
    Item item = domain.getItem("Car 1");
    List<ItemAttribute> list = new ArrayList<ItemAttribute>();
    list.add(new ItemAttribute("dealer", "Tom the dealer", false));
    list.add(new ItemAttribute("dealer", "My local Mercedes",
        false));
    item.putAttributes(list);

    Item saved_item = domain.getItem("Car 1");
    for (ItemAttribute attr : saved_item.getAttributes()) {
        System.out.println("  " + attr.getName() + " = "
        + attr.getValue());
    }
} catch (SDBException ex) {
    System.out.println(ex.getMessage());
}
```

Storing multiple values in a single attribute with PHP

You can specify a multi-value value by assigning an array to the `value` such as in the `color` attribute line in the following code:

```
$sdb = new SimpleDB(awsAccessKey, awsSecretKey); // create connection

$item_name = "car1";

// Add an attribute
$putAttributesRequest["make"] = array("value" => "BMW");

// Add an attribute with multiple values
$putAttributesRequest["color"] =
    array("value" => array("grey","red"));
$putAttributesRequest["year"] = array("value" => "2008");

// Replace existing values
$putAttributesRequest["desc"] = array("value" => "Sedan",
    "replace" => "true");

$putAttributesRequest["model"] = array("value" => "530i");

print_r($sdb->
    putAttributes($domain,$item_name,$putAttributesRequest));
$putAttributesRequest["color"] =
    array("value" => array("grey","red"));
```

This line is adding two values to a single attribute. The result of this line depends on the original value of the attribute. The following table examines the before and after of this line.

Before	After (replace=true)
No color	color = grey and color = red for item car1
color = grey and color = red for item car1	color = grey and color = red for item car1
color = blue for item car1	color = blue and color = grey and color = red for item car1

Storing multiple values in a single attribute with Python

A single attribute in SimpleDB can have multiple values. In this section we will explore this feature using Python.

```
>>> myitem1.add_value('dealer','Tom the dealer, My local Mercedes')
>>>
>>> myitem1.save()
>>>
>>> myitem1
{u'color': u'White', u'make': u'Mercedes', 'dealer': 'Tom the dealer, My
local Mercedes', 'year': '2009'}
>>>
>>> myitem2.add_value('dealer','Tom the dealer')
>>>
>>> myitem2.save()
>>>
>>> myitem2
{u'color': u'Black', u'make': u'BMW', 'dealer': 'Tom the dealer'}
>>>
>>>
```

In this code sample, we added two different values for the dealer attribute.

You can store multiple values for an attribute by comma-separating the different values when adding or updating the attribute. Do not let the comma-separated values fool you into thinking that SimpleDB just stores the multiple values that way and you will need to do string parsing on your side while querying for matching values. SimpleDB actually stores and indexes these multiple values for the attribute in such a way as to make it very simple to query and retrieve them. They are stored conceptually as two different dealer attributes in our example data, but linked correctly with the right item.

The following figure gives a simple visualization of how multiple values are stored by SimpleDB internally. When you query for an attribute that has multiple values, the attribute is returned with multiple values that are comma-separated. However, internally SimpleDB stores the multiple values for an attribute as two similarly-named attributes with different values.

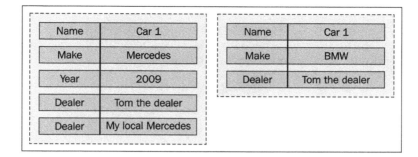

We will discuss querying in detail in *Chapter 6, Querying*, and we will see how simple SimpleDB makes it to search and retrieve your multi-valued attributes.

Constraints on values of a SimpleDB item

A value stored in an attribute must follow these restrictions:

- The length of the value cannot be more than 1024 bytes.
- The value must only use characters that are UTF-8 characters, which are valid in XML documents. Control characters and any sequences that are not valid in XML are not allowed for use as part of the value. This is true for SOAP requests. Invalid XML characters inserted when using the REST API will be returned as base64-encoded values when retrieving an item later.

Consistent Read and Conditional Put / Delete announcement

Two key enhancements were announced on February 24, 2010 to SimpleDB: Consistent Read for `getAttributes`/Select and Conditional Put/Delete.

ConsistentRead = true for getAttributes and Select

Consistent Read enables you to get the most recent values bypassing the eventual consistency system. Consistent Read should not be used as a way to bypass eventual consistency, but is very useful in counters and code where reading the most recent value is critical.

In the following PHP sample, we create an item with the date/time and immediately use a `getAttributes` with `ConsistentRead=true`, then a normal `getAttributes`. The Consistent Read will return the just-updated value while the eventual consistency read will usually return the old value.

```php
$sdb = new SimpleDB(awsAccessKey, awsSecretKey);
  // create connection
$domain = "testread";
  // Check that the domain exists
$domainmd = $sdb->domainMetadata($domain);
echo("Domain $domain Metadata requested<br>");
echo("BoxUsage: ".$sdb->BoxUsage." = "
    . SimpleDB::displayUsage($sdb->BoxUsage)."<p>");

if (!$domainmd) { // Create if it does not exist
    if($sdb->createDomain($domain)) {
        echo("Domain $domain created<br>");
        echo("BoxUsage: ".$sdb->BoxUsage." = "
            . SimpleDB::displayUsage($sdb->BoxUsage)."<p>");
    }
}
// build array of items and attribute/value pairs
$putAttributesRequest = array();

$item_name = "testitem";
echo "putAttributes() record 'testitem'<br>";
$thetime = Time();  // get current time/date
$now = SimpleDB::encodeDateTime($thetime);
echo("ISO8601 format: $now &lt;-- NEW TIME<br>");

$putAttributesRequest["datetime"] =
    array("value" => $now, "replace" => "true");
  // store date time replace = true

// Put the latest date/time
$rest = $sdb->
    putAttributes($domain,$item_name,$putAttributesRequest);
if ($rest) {
    echo("Record $item_name created<br>");
    echo("BoxUsage: ".$sdb->BoxUsage." = "
        . SimpleDB::displayUsage($sdb->BoxUsage)."<br>");
} else {
    echo("Record $item_name FAILED<br>");
    echo("ErrorCode: ".$sdb->ErrorCode."<p>");
}

// Read back with ConsistentRead as true (fourth parameter)
$rest = $sdb->getAttributes($domain,$item_name,null,true);
```

```
if ($rest) {
    echo "<br>getAttributes for $item_name ConsistentRead=True<br>";
    $datetime = $rest["datetime"];
    if ($now == $datetime) {
        echo "DateTime: $datetime &lt;-- NEW TIME<br>";
    } else {
    echo "DateTime: $datetime <b>&lt;-- OLD TIME </b><br>";
    }
    echo("BoxUsage: ".$sdb->BoxUsage." = "
        . SimpleDB::displayUsage($sdb->BoxUsage)."<br>");
} else {
    echo("Listing FAILED<br>");
    echo("ErrorCode: ".$sdb->ErrorCode."<p>");
}

// Normal eventual consistency read
$rest = $sdb->getAttributes($domain,$item_name);
if ($rest) {
    echo "<br>getAttributes for $item_name<br>";
    $now = $rest["datetime"];
    if ($thetime == $datetime) {
        echo "DateTime: $datetime &lt;-- NEW TIME<br>";
    } else {
    echo "DateTime: $datetime <b>&lt;-- OLD TIME </b><br>";
    }
    echo("BoxUsage: ".$sdb->BoxUsage." = "
        . SimpleDB::displayUsage($sdb->BoxUsage)."<br>");
    } else {
    echo("Listing FAILED<br>");
    echo("ErrorCode: ".$sdb->ErrorCode."<p>");
}
```

The program when run returns:

```
putAttributes() record 'testitem'
ISO8601 format: 2010-02-27T20:01:09-04:00 <-- NEW TIME
Record testitem created
BoxUsage: 0.0000219909 = 22.0 muH

getAttributes for testitem ConsistentRead=True
DateTime: 2010-02-27T20:01:09-04:00 <-- NEW TIME
BoxUsage: 0.0000093222 = 9.3 muH

getAttributes for testitem
DateTime: 2010-02-27T20:01:09-04:00 <-- OLD TIME
BoxUsage: 0.0000093222 = 9.3 muH

    Domain: testread, item: testitem
```

In review, this program performed the following steps:

1. Set the `datetime` attribute to `2010-02-27T20:01:09-04:00`.

2. Read `datetime` using `getAttributes` with `ConsistentRead=true`. Returns `2010-02-27T20:01:09-04:00`.

3. Read `datetime` using `getAttributes`. Returns `2010-02-27T20:01:09-04:00 <-- OLD TIME`.

4. So using `ConsistentRead = true` with `getAttributes` and `Select` will return the most recent value bypassing eventual consistency.

Conditional Put / Delete

Conditional Put/Delete is being able to check for an existing condition before doing the put or delete. The check uses `ConsistentRead=true` so you are basing the decision on the most recent data.

Conditional Put allows you to add or replace one or more attributes to an item if the consistent value of a single-valued attribute has a specific value or does not exist. It is important to note that the condition is based on a single attribute value. It cannot be used with an attribute with multiple values. Conditional Delete is the same except you allow a delete rather than a put.

In this example, the program will fetch the attributes for a specific item `car3` and display them. Then it will try a delete with a condition that will fail, then a delete with a condition that will work.

```
$sdb = new SimpleDB(awsAccessKey, awsSecretKey);
  // create connection
$domain = "car-s";
$item_name = "car3";
$rest = $sdb->getAttributes($domain,$item_name);
if ($rest) {
    echo "<b>getAttributes for $item_name</b><pre>";
    print_r($rest);
    echo "</pre>";
    echo("RequestId: ".$sdb->RequestId."<br>");
    echo("BoxUsage: ".$sdb->BoxUsage." = " .
SimpleDB::displayUsage($sdb->BoxUsage)."<p>");
} else {
    echo("Listing FAILED<br>");
    echo("ErrorCode: ".$sdb->ErrorCode."<p>");
}
```

```
echo "<b>deleteAttributes item $item_name IF make =
    Acura (will fail)</b><pre>";
$putExists["make"] = array("value" => "Acura");
  // check if make = Acura
$rest=$sdb->deleteAttributes($domain,$item_name,null,$putExists);
  // delete whole record
if ($rest) {
    echo("Record $item_name updated<br>");
    echo("BoxUsage: ".$sdb->BoxUsage." = "
        . SimpleDB::displayUsage($sdb->BoxUsage)."<p>");
} else {
    echo("Record $item_name FAILED<br>");
    echo("ErrorCode: ".$sdb->ErrorCode."<p>");
}

unset($putExists);
echo "<b>deleteAttributes item $item_name
    IF make = Lexus (will succeed)</b><pre>";
$putExists["make"] = array("value" => "Lexus");
  // check if make = Acura
$rest=$sdb->deleteAttributes($domain,$item_name,null,$putExists);
  // delete whole record
if ($rest) {
    echo("Record $item_name updated<br>");
    echo("BoxUsage: ".$sdb->BoxUsage." = " .
SimpleDB::displayUsage($sdb->BoxUsage)."<p>");
} else {
    echo("Record $item_name FAILED<br>");
    echo("ErrorCode: ".$sdb->ErrorCode."<p>");
}
```

First, run seventh menu item (create multiple records with `batchPutAttributes` in car-s) to create the items.

The program when run returns:

```
getAttributes for car3
Array
(
    [color] => Array
        (
            [0] => Blue
            [1] => Red
        )

    [year] => 2008
```

```
        [make] => Lexus
)
RequestId: 16a1a20b-d42a-15d5-e002-33dc1197885e
BoxUsage: 0.0000093382 = 9.3 muH
deleteAttributes item car3 IF make = Acura (will fail)
Record car3 FAILED
ErrorCode: ConditionalCheckFailed
deleteAttributes item car3 IF make = Lexus (will succeed)
Record car3 updated
BoxUsage: 0.0000219907 = 22.0 muH
```

In review, the program did the following steps:

1. Fetch the attributes for item car3.

2. Delete car3 if make=Acura. As the make is Lexus this delete will fail.

3. Delete car3 if make=Lexus. This is the correct make so the item is deleted.

The expanded Java and Python APIs are not available as of the writing of the book. The concepts will be identical in those interfaces; the calls will just differ.

Summary

In this chapter, we discussed the SimpleDB model in detail. We explored the different methods for interacting with a domain, its items, and their attributes. We learned about the domain metadata. We also reviewed the various constraints imposed by SimpleDB on domains, items, and attributes. In the next chapter, we are going to review data types and how to encode and decode them easily into string data that is the native storage type for SimpleDB.

5
Data Types

SimpleDB stores the values for all attributes in your items as UTF-8 strings. This means that all comparisons between attributes to determine order or to match search criteria will be done lexicographically. Your application needs to be aware of this fact and encode data correctly before saving it to SimpleDB and decode the data correctly on retrieval from SimpleDB. Coding of dates and numbers is necessary in SimpleDB if the application will search for a value or sort on the values. All values in SimpleDB are treated as case-sensitive and must be taken into consideration. SimpleDB leaves the data type conversions to the developer, and thus provides you with a lot of flexibility in dealing with your data that is to be stored in SimpleDB. In this chapter, we will look at different kinds of data types and the encoding and decoding strategies to be used when storing and retrieving them from SimpleDB.

In this chapter, we will cover:

- Lexicographical comparison
- Storing numbers
- Storing dates
- Storing Boolean values
- Storing XML-restricted characters

What is lexicographical comparison?

Lexicographical comparison is a technique used for sorting words alphabetically by comparing the characters in a string sequentially from left to right. The order of precedence used when comparing the characters in a string is:

1. Digits
2. Uppercase letters
3. Lowercase letters

In the following figure, we display how a lexicographical comparison works when comparing each set of strings:

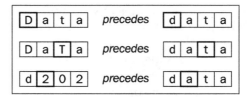

Here, the box with the bold outline indicates the letter that decides the precedence when comparing these two strings. When doing a comparison, you start on the left side and go from left to right, one letter at a time, and compare the letters at that position. If they are the same, you move on to the next letter. However, if the letters do not match, you can decide on which letter is greater and at that point you have an answer for the lexicographical comparison.

The resulting alphabetic list is:

- d2t2
- Data
- daTa
- data

Storing numeric values

Attributes that store number values, which need to be sorted or compared, need to use the technique of zero padding so that they work correctly when using lexicographical comparison. If you store two number values 2 and 10, a normal lexicographical comparison will result in the value 2 being greater than 10. This is, of course, not exactly what you would expect to get when comparing these values as numbers.

 The solution is to store the number values with padding for the right number of digits.

We will store 2 as 02. Now a lexicographical comparison between 02 and 10 will return what you expect! In order to pad your data correctly, you need to know the limits of the number values that will be stored. If you know how large a number is to be stored, you can then pad each number that is being stored in your attributes with the right number of digits.

If you need to store negative numbers as attribute values and want to compare them, then storing them with just a zero padding will not work. In this case, you need to know the entire range of numbers that will be stored. Once you know the range, choose an offset larger than the smallest expected negative number and add it to all the numbers. This will of course change all of the negative numbers into positive numbers. Now you can use the same zero padding technique as before, prior to saving the data values into SimpleDB. This will ensure that the numbers are compared in a lexicographically correct manner. The same procedure needs to be applied in a reverse fashion when retrieving the data values from SimpleDB. If you have an expected dataset consisting of the following numbers:

```
21, 3, -12345, 9876, 278268, -341
```

Sorting these numbers as strings yields:

```
-12345
```

```
21
```

```
278268
```

```
3
```

```
-341
```

```
9876
```

Clearly, these are not the expected results.

If you know that the smallest expected negative number in your set is likely to be -20,000, you can safely use an offset of say 1,00,000 and add it to the numbers.

```
100021, 100003, 087655, 109876, 378268, 099659
```

Sorting these numbers as strings yields:

087655 (-12345)

099659 (-341)

100003 (3)

100021 (21)

109876 (9876)

378268 (278268)

Storing numeric values with Java

Typica has a `DataUtils` class that provides several utility functions that can be used for encoding and decoding values to form zero-padded strings. Here are two methods provided by Typica for encoding and decoding integers.

```java
public static String encodeZeroPadding(int number, int maxNumDigits) {
    String integerString = Integer.toString(number);
    int numZeroes = maxNumDigits - integerString.length();
    StringBuffer strBuffer = new StringBuffer(numZeroes +
integerString.length());
    for (int i = 0; i < numZeroes; i++) {
        strBuffer.insert(i, '0');
    }
    strBuffer.append(integerString);
    return strBuffer.toString();
}
public static int decodeZeroPaddingInt(String value) {
    return Integer.parseInt(value, 10);
}
```

There are several other utility methods for dealing with the storage of long numbers as zero-padded values.

Storing numeric values with PHP

The SDB-PHP library has two functions for encoding and decoding numbers for the database. Function `encodeNum` encodes a number while `decodeNum` decodes the number. The functions are configured by three constants in `config.inc.php`:

1. `awsNumLength`: Total number of digits to store a number.

2. `awsNumDecimals`: Number of decimal places.

3. `awsNumNegOffset`: Negative number offset to add (abs value of minimum negative number).

```php
if (!class_exists('SimpleDB')) require_once('sdb.php');
echo("<b>Basic Conversion</b> (Use defined config)<br>");
echo("<table border=1>");
echo("<tr><th>Original</th><th>Encoded</th><th>Decoded</th></
tr>");
$testvals = array(27, 2.287, 12584.5963, -5, -5.875, -100000);
foreach ($testvals as $t) {
    $e = SimpleDB::encodeNum($t);
    $d = SimpleDB::decodeNum($e);
    echo("<tr><td>$t</td><td>$e</td><td>$d</td></tr>");
}
echo("</table>");
echo("<br><b>Advanced Conversion</b> (Override defined
config)<br>");
echo('$sdb->encodeNum(27, 15, 4, 10000000000)<br>');
echo("27= ".SimpleDB::encodeNum(27, 15, 4, 10000000000)."<p>");
```

Assuming these values as defined in `config.ini.php`:

```php
define('awsNumLength', 10); // Total length
define('awsNumDecimals', 2); // Number of decimals
define('awsNumNegOffset', 100000000); // Negative number offset
```

This code outputs:

Basic Conversion (Use defined configuration)

Original	Encoded	Decoded
27	0100002700	27
2.287	0100000229	2.29
12584.5963	0101258460	12584.6
-5	0099999500	-5
-5.875	0099999412	-5.88
-100000	0090000000	-100000

Several values were rounded to two decimal places.

The standard settings on encode and decode can also be overridden with additional parameters.

```
function encodeNum($input, $numLen = awsNumLength,
                   $numDec = awsNumDecimals,
                   $numOffset = awsNumNegOffset)
function decodeNum($input, $numDec = awsNumDecimals,
                   $numOffset = awsNumNegOffset)
```

Storing numeric values with Python

You can encode and decode positive and negative integers using these simple Python functions. The offset used is `2147483648`, which is the number 231, which should be large enough for all the integers. These functions can be saved in the Python file that contains your code for encoding and decoding integers.

```
def encode_int(value):
    value = int(value)
    value += 2147483648
    return '%010d' % value
def decode_int(value):
    value = int(value)
    value -= 2147483648
    return int(value)
```

Here are some results from encoding and decoding a few integers. You can also type the aforementioned functions into a Python console session, and then use the functions as shown below:

```
>>>
>>> encode_int(123409)
'2147607057'
>>>
>>> encode_int(-123409)
'2147360239'
>>>
>>> decode_int(2147607057)
123409
>>>
```

```
>>> decode_int(2147360239)
-123409
>>>
```

If the numbers that you need to store are larger than just integers, you can use a different set of methods, and an offset of 9223372036854775808.

```
def encode_long(value):
    value = long(value)
    value += 9223372036854775808
    return '%020d' % value

def decode_long(value):
    value = long(value)
    value -= 9223372036854775808
    return value
```

Here are some results from encoding and decoding a few long numbers:

```
>>>
>>> encode_long(9223372036854775808)
'18446744073709551616'
>>>
>>> encode_long(-776627963145224200)
'08446744073709551608'
>>>
>>> decode_long(8446744073709551608)
-776627963145224200L
>>>
```

Storing date values

Date values are much more difficult to compare lexicographically, as the formats are so different and there is no guarantee that the significant units will be in the right position in the date string. It is possible to store the date as the number of epoch seconds since January 1, 1970. This will work but is a bit cumbersome, as the stored number is not at all readable and you will need to convert it to another meaningful date format to make any sense of it.

 A better solution is to use a date format that is friendly to a lexicographical comparison—**ISO8601**.

ISO8601 is a format that is also being used by some of the Amazon Web Services. It is an international standard for representing date formats in an unambiguous way while making comparisons between two dates simpler. The date and time values are organized from the most to the least significant components: year, month (or week), day, hour, minute, second, and fraction of second. The time representation possesses a lexicographical order that corresponds to chronological order.

The formats for an ISO8601 date are as follows:

- **Year**: YYYY (2009)
- **Year and month**: YYYY-MM (2009-10)
- **Complete date**: YYYY-MM-DD (2009-10-04)
- **Complete date plus hours and minutes**:
  YYYY-MM-DDThh:mmTZD
  (2009-10-04T19:00+01:00)
- **Complete date plus hours, minutes, and seconds**:
  YYYY-MM-DDThh:mm:ssTZD
  (2009-10-04T19:00:30+01:00)
- **Complete date plus hours, minutes, seconds and a decimal fraction of a second**:
  YYYY-MM-DDThh:mm:ss.sTZD
  (2009-10-04T19:00:30.45+01:00)

The letters used in the above format are:

- **YYYY**: Four-digit year
- **MM**: Two-digit month (01 = January, and so on)
- **DD**: Two-digit day of month (01 through 31)
- **hh**: Two digits of hour (00 through 23, a.m./p.m. NOT allowed)
- **mm**: Two digits of minute (00 through 59)
- **ss**: Two digits of second (00 through 59)
- **s**: One or more digits representing a decimal fraction of a second
- **TZD**: Time zone designator (Z or +hh:mm or -hh:mm)

Our recommendation would be to ideally store times as **Coordinated Universal Time (UTC)** times, and not as local times. Each ISO8601 date must have all of these components present in one of these formats. The T that appears in the date string indicates the beginning of the time element. The time zones are handled in two different ways:

- Times can be expressed in UTC, with a special UTC designator ("Z"). For instance, 2009-10-04T19:00:00Z, represents a time in UTC.

- Times can be expressed in local time, together with a time zone offset in hours and minutes. A time zone offset of "+hh:mm" indicates that the date/time uses a local time zone which is "hh" hours and "mm" minutes ahead of UTC. A time zone offset of "-hh:mm" indicates that the date/time uses a local time zone which is "hh" hours and "mm" minutes behind UTC. For instance, 2009-10-04T14:00:00-05:00 is the same as the earlier time, except that it is in the US Eastern Time Zone.

Storing date values with Java

Typica provides the following two methods for encoding and decoding date values in Java:

```java
public static String encodeDate(Date date) {
    SimpleDateFormat dateFormatter = new
        SimpleDateFormat(dateFormat);
    String result = dateFormatter.format(date);
    return result.substring(0, result.length() - 2)
        + ":" + result.substring(result.length() - 2);
}
public static Date decodeDate(String value) throws ParseException {
    String javaValue = value.substring(0, value.length() - 3)
        + value.substring(value.length() - 2);
    SimpleDateFormat dateFormatter = new
        SimpleDateFormat(dateFormat);
    return dateFormatter.parse(javaValue);
}
```

Storing date values with PHP

Two functions in the SimpleDB PHP library provide date/time encoding and decoding. Similar to the numeric functions they support sorting by date/time.

Input to encodeDateTime is a Unix timestamp while decodeDateTime returns a Unix timestamp.

```
if (!class_exists('SimpleDB')) require_once('sdb.php');

$thetime = Time();  // get current time/date

echo("Timecode: $thetime<br>");

$now = SimpleDB::encodeDateTime($thetime);
echo("ISO8601 format: $now using encodeDateTime()<br>");

$dt = SimpleDB::decodeDateTime($now);

echo("Timecode: $dt using decodeDateTime()<p>");
```

This will return:

```
Timecode: 1267728809
ISO8601 format: 2010-03-04T14:53:29-04:00 using encodeDateTime()
Timecode: 1267728809 using decodeDateTime()
```

Storing date values with Python

You can encode and decode dates into an ISO8601 format easily using these Python methods. You can once again type these methods into a Python console session or use them in a Python file that contains your date storage code.

```
from datetime import datetime

def encode_datetime(value):
        return value.strftime('%Y-%m-%dT%H:%M:%SZ')

    def decode_datetime(value):
        return datetime.strptime(value,'%Y-%m-%dT%H:%M:%SZ')
```

The encode_datetime() method takes a string value and formats it using the ISO8601 format while the decode_datetime() method does the reverse and translates an ISO8601 formatted string into a date object.

We can use these two functions as shown following to encode and decode the current time into and out of ISO8601 format in Python.

```
>>>
>>> encode_datetime(datetime.utcnow())
'2009-09-30T14:44:57Z'
>>>
>>>
>>> mydate = datetime.utcnow()
>>>
>>> mydate
datetime.datetime(2009, 9, 30, 14, 45, 41, 255445)
```

```
>>>
>>> encode_datetime(mydate)
'2009-09-30T14:45:41Z'
>>>
>>> decode_datetime('2009-09-30T14:45:41Z')
datetime.datetime(2009, 9, 30, 14, 45, 41)
>>>
```

Storing Boolean values

Booleans are very commonly used for storing binary values. You can either choose to store them as a simple 0 or 1 in SimpleDB or store them in a slightly more readable way as the string values true and false.

Storing Boolean values with Java

Here are two simple methods to convert values from a Boolean to a string and vice versa:

- ```
  public String encodeBoolean(boolean valueToEncode) {
      return new Boolean(valueToEncode).toString();
  }
  ```
- ```
  public boolean decodeBoolean(String encodedValue) {
      return encodedValue.equalsIgnoreCase("true");
  }
  ```

Storing Boolean values with PHP

These functions are in the SimpleDB PHP library. Boolean true is stored as the string true while false is stored as the string false. The following functions isolate the program from the stored value so that as an example 1 and 0 could be used for true and false instead:

```
public function encodeBoolean($input) {
  if ($input) {
    return "true";
  } else {
    return "false";
  }
}
public function decodeBoolean($input) {
  if (strtolower($input)=="true") {
```

```
      return true;
   } else {
      return false;
   }
}
```

They can be accessed as follows:

```
if (!class_exists('SimpleDB')) require_once('sdb.php');

$val1 = true;
$val2 = false;

$enval1 = SimpleDB::encodeBoolean($val1);
$enval2 = SimpleDB::encodeBoolean($val2);

$bkval1 = SimpleDB::decodeBoolean($enval1);
$bkval2 = SimpleDB::decodeBoolean($enval2);

echo("$val1 to $enval1 back $bkval1<br>");
echo("$val2 to $enval2 back $bkval2<p>");
```

This code returns:

```
1 to true back 1
to false back
```

Storing Boolean values with Python

You can enter these methods in a Python file to use them or enter them at the Python console and use them in a console session.

```
def encode_bool(value):
    if value == True:
        return 'true'
    else:
        return 'false'
def decode_bool(value):
    if value.lower() == 'true':
        return True
    else:
        return False
```

These two methods store Python Booleans as string values and translate them into Python Booleans `True` or `False`, as and when required. Here is an example showing how to use these two methods in a Python console session:

```
>>>
>>> encode_bool(True)
'true'
>>>>>> encode_bool(False)
'false'
>>>
>>> decode_bool('true')
True
>>> decode_bool('false')
False
>>>
>>> decode_bool('False')
False
>>>
```

XML-restricted characters

All interaction with SimpleDB is in the form of XML documents that contain the requests. The underlying libraries that are used for communicating with SimpleDB will usually take care of the creation and parsing of these XML documents and present the results to you in a format specific to the library. In our case, boto is translating the XML responses from SimpleDB into simple Python objects that can be consumed by our application. The use of XML implies that you cannot send across any Unicode characters as a part of your data values that are invalid XML characters. You can insert invalid XML characters using the ReST API and they will be stored in SimpleDB, and will be automatically encoded as base64 strings when retrieved. If you do need to store these characters in SimpleDB, a simple way of doing that would be to encode these characters using a base64 encoding, and then store them in SimpleDB. You will, of course, need to decode them after retrieval before use in your application.

Base64 is a way to encode any kind of data into plain ASCII text. Base64 encoding takes three bytes of character data (three ASCII characters or one and a half UNICODE characters) and converts it into four bytes of data from the universal character set. It does the conversion in two steps:

1. It first converts three bytes into four numbers of six bits each. Even though each character in the ASCII standard consists of seven bits, base64 encoding only uses 6 bits. This ensures that base64 encoded data can be printed and that it is human-readable.

2. These numbers are then converted into ASCII characters using the character set shown in the following table.

Base64 Encoding Character Set

Value	Encoding	Value	Encoding	Value	Encoding	Value	Encoding
0	A	16	Q	32	g	48	w
1	B	17	R	33	h	49	x
2	C	18	S	34	I	50	y
3	D	19	T	35	j	51	z
4	E	20	U	36	k	52	0
5	F	21	V	37	l	53	1
6	G	22	W	38	m	54	2
7	H	23	X	39	n	55	3
8	I	24	Y	40	o	56	4
9	J	25	Z	41	p	57	5
10	K	26	a	42	q	58	6
11	L	27	b	43	r	59	7
12	M	28	c	44	s	60	8
13	N	29	d	45	t	61	9
14	O	30	e	46	u	62	+
15	P	31	f	47	v	63	/

Using base64 values with Java

Currently the `DataUtils` class does not include any methods for base64 encoding values, but it is quite simple to do this using the **commons codec** project from Apache. You can download a JAR version of the library from the website `http://commons.apache.org/codec/download_codec.cgi`. Here are two simple methods in Java that use the codec JAR to do base64 encoding and decoding.

```
public static String encodeBase64(String valueToEncode) throws
EncoderException {
    Base64 base64 = new Base64();
    return base64.encode(valueToEncode).toString();
}

public static String decodeBase64(String encodedValue) throws
DecoderException {
    Base64 base64 = new Base64();
    return base64.decode(encodedValue).toString();
}
```

Using base64 values with PHP

Here are two simple functions in the SimpleDB library that can be used for encoding and decoding characters using base64 in PHP. While these functions are trivial, they isolate the program from how the data is stored.

```
public function encodeBase64($input) {
    return base64_encode($input);
}

public function decodeBase64($input) {
    return base64_decode($input);
}
```

Here is an example of using the functions:

```
if (!class_exists('SimpleDB')) require_once('sdb.php');
$val = "abcdefghijklmnopqrstuvwxyz'\/*@#$%^&()";
$enval = SimpleDB::encodeBase64($val);
$bkval = SimpleDB::decodeBase64($enval);
echo("Input: $val<p>Base64: $enval<p>Decoded: $bkval<p>");
```

This code returns:

Input: abcdefghijklmnopqrstuvwxyz'\/*@#$%^&()

Base64: YWJjZGVmZ2hpamtsbW5vcHFyc3R1dnd4eXonXC8qQCMkJV4mKCk=

Decoded: abcdefghijklmnopqrstuvwxyz'\/*@#$%^&()

Using base64 values with Python

Here are two simple methods that can be used for encoding and decoding characters using base64 in Python:

```
import base64
def encode_b64_value(value):
    return base64.encodestring(value)

def decode_b64_value(value):
    return base64.decodestring(value)
```

The `encode_b64_value()` method takes string and encodes it to base64 using the built-in Python base64 module. The `decode_b64_value()` method does the reverse and decodes a base64-encoded string into a plain string value. You can use these two methods for encoding and decoding invalid characters such as the angled brackets.

```
>>>
>>> encode_b64_value('<mytag>hello</mytag>')
'PG15dGFnPmhlbGxvPC9teXRhZz4=\n'
>>>
>>> decode_b64_value('PG15dGFnPmhlbGxvPC9teXRhZz4=\n')
'<mytag>hello</mytag>'
>>>
```

Summary

In this chapter, we discussed the techniques needed for storing different data types in SimpleDB. We explored a technique for storing numbers, Boolean values, and dates. We also discussed XML-restricted characters, and encoding them using base64 encoding. In the next chapter, we are going to review querying for your data stored in SimpleDB.

6
Querying

We have our data stored nicely in SimpleDB domains. Now we are going to learn the different ways to retrieve the stored data. Most of us are used to using **Structured Query Language (SQL)** for retrieving data from relational databases. SimpleDB uses a select syntax that is very similar to its counterpart in SQL for the queries. In this chapter, we will explore the query syntax provided by SimpleDB with a lot of samples and learn about:

- The basic select syntax
- Quoting values inside select expressions
- Predicates in select expressions
- Comparison operators
- Set operations
- Sorting
- Counting the results from SimpleDB queries
- Queries on multi-valued attributes
- `GetAttributes`

Sample data

We are going to use songs as our dataset. The following screenshot shows a section of my iTunes library and its song-listing window. We are going to take this information and store it in SimpleDB, and then run queries against this data.

The sample data shown in this screenshot is now displayed in table form, and we will be storing this data in SimpleDB.

Item name	Song	Artist	Year	Genre	Rating
112222222	My Way	Frank Sinatra	2002	Easy Listening	**** 4 stars Excellent
089997979	Hotel California	Gipsy Kings		World	****
982411114	Geraldine	Glasvegas	2008	Rock Alternative	*****
6767969119	Transmission	Joy Division	1981	Alternative	***** Excellent
6721309888	Guzarish	Ghazini	2008	Bollywood	Not rated Awful
0923424244	So What	Miles Davis	1959	Jazz	***** Wow!
5697878778	Allison	Pixies	1990	Alternative	**** 4 stars

Item name	Song	Artist	Year	Genre	Rating
7233929292	Pride	Syntax		Electronic Alternative	***** Excellent
5656600009	Acapulco	Neil Diamond	1980	Soundtrack	* 1 star Avoid
1002380899	Scream in Blue	Midnight Oil	1983	Rock	*** 3 stars
1045845425	You're a Strange Animal	Gowan	1985	Rock	****

Loading the sample data

We are going to create a new SimpleDB domain called songs and load the sample data shown in the table into the domain. We will then use this sample data to explore the support for querying SimpleDB.

Importing the sample data with Java

We will first create a domain named songs using **Typica**.

```
SimpleDB sdb = new SimpleDB(awsAccessId, awsSecretKey, true);
try {
    Domain domain = sdb.createDomain("songs");
    System.out.println(domain.getName());

} catch (SDBException ex) {
    System.out.println(ex.getMessage());
}
```

Now let's import data into this newly created domain.

```
SimpleDB sdb = new SimpleDB(awsAccessId, awsSecretKey, true);
try {
    Domain domain = sdb.getDomain("songs");
    Item item = domain.getItem("112222222");
    List<ItemAttribute> list = new ArrayList<ItemAttribute>();
    list.add(new ItemAttribute("Song", "My Way", false));
    list.add(new ItemAttribute("Artist", "Frank Sinatra", false));
    list.add(new ItemAttribute("Year", "2002", false));
    list.add(new ItemAttribute("Genre", "Easy Listening", false));
    list.add(new ItemAttribute("Rating", "****", false));
    list.add(new ItemAttribute("Rating", "4 stars", false));
```

```
list.add(new ItemAttribute("Rating", "Excellent", false));
item.putAttributes(list);

item = domain.getItem("089997979");
list = new ArrayList<ItemAttribute>();
list.add(new ItemAttribute("Song", "Hotel California", false));
list.add(new ItemAttribute("Artist", "Gipsy Kings", false));
list.add(new ItemAttribute("Genre", "World", false));
list.add(new ItemAttribute("Rating", "****", false));
item.putAttributes(list);

item = domain.getItem("982411114");
list = new ArrayList<ItemAttribute>();
list.add(new ItemAttribute("Song", "Geraldine", false));
list.add(new ItemAttribute("Artist", "Glasvegas", false));
list.add(new ItemAttribute("Year", "2008", false));
list.add(new ItemAttribute("Genre", "Rock", false));
list.add(new ItemAttribute("Genre", "Alternative", false));
list.add(new ItemAttribute("Rating", "*****", false));
item.putAttributes(list);

item = domain.getItem("6767969119");
list = new ArrayList<ItemAttribute>();
list.add(new ItemAttribute("Song", "Transmission", false));
list.add(new ItemAttribute("Artist", "Joy Division", false));
list.add(new ItemAttribute("Year", "1981", false));
list.add(new ItemAttribute("Genre", "Alternative", false));
list.add(new ItemAttribute("Rating", "*****", false));
list.add(new ItemAttribute("Rating", "Excellent", false));
item.putAttributes(list);

item = domain.getItem("6721309888");
list = new ArrayList<ItemAttribute>();
list.add(new ItemAttribute("Song", "Guzarish", false));
list.add(new ItemAttribute("Artist", "Ghazini", false));
list.add(new ItemAttribute("Year", "2008", false));
list.add(new ItemAttribute("Genre", "Bollywood", false));
list.add(new ItemAttribute("Rating", "Not rated", false));
list.add(new ItemAttribute("Rating", "Awful", false));
item.putAttributes(list);

item = domain.getItem("0923424244");
list = new ArrayList<ItemAttribute>();
list.add(new ItemAttribute("Song", "So What", false));
list.add(new ItemAttribute("Artist", "Miles Davis", false));
list.add(new ItemAttribute("Year", "1959", false));
list.add(new ItemAttribute("Genre", "Jazz", false));
list.add(new ItemAttribute("Rating", "*****", false));
```

```
    list.add(new ItemAttribute("Rating", "Wow!", false));
    item.putAttributes(list);

    item = domain.getItem("5697878778");
    list = new ArrayList<ItemAttribute>();
    list.add(new ItemAttribute("Song", "Allison", false));
    list.add(new ItemAttribute("Artist", "Pixies", false));
    list.add(new ItemAttribute("Year", "1990", false));
    list.add(new ItemAttribute("Genre", "Alternative", false));
    list.add(new ItemAttribute("Rating", "****", false));
    list.add(new ItemAttribute("Rating", "4 stars", false));
    item.putAttributes(list);

    item = domain.getItem("7233929292");
    list = new ArrayList<ItemAttribute>();
    list.add(new ItemAttribute("Song", "Pride", false));
    list.add(new ItemAttribute("Artist", "Syntax", false));
    list.add(new ItemAttribute("Genre", "Electronic", false));
    list.add(new ItemAttribute("Genre", "Alternative", false));
    list.add(new ItemAttribute("Rating", "*****", false));
    list.add(new ItemAttribute("Rating", "Excellent", false));
    item.putAttributes(list);

    item = domain.getItem("5656600009");
    list = new ArrayList<ItemAttribute>();
    list.add(new ItemAttribute("Song", "Acapulco", false));
    list.add(new ItemAttribute("Artist", "Neil Diamond", false));
    list.add(new ItemAttribute("Year", "1980", false));
    list.add(new ItemAttribute("Genre", "Soundtrack", false));
    list.add(new ItemAttribute("Rating", "*", false));
    list.add(new ItemAttribute("Rating", "1 star", false));
    list.add(new ItemAttribute("Rating", "Avoid", false));
    item.putAttributes(list);

    item = domain.getItem("1002380899");
    list = new ArrayList<ItemAttribute>();
    list.add(new ItemAttribute("Song", "Scream in Blue", false));
    list.add(new ItemAttribute("Artist", "Midnight Oil", false));
    list.add(new ItemAttribute("Year", "1983", false));
    list.add(new ItemAttribute("Genre", "Rock", false));
    list.add(new ItemAttribute("Rating", "***", false));
    list.add(new ItemAttribute("Rating", "3 stars", false));
    item.putAttributes(list);

    item = domain.getItem("1045845425");
    list = new ArrayList<ItemAttribute>();
    list.add(new ItemAttribute("Song", "You're a Strange Animal",
false));
```

```
        list.add(new ItemAttribute("Artist", "Gowan", false));
        list.add(new ItemAttribute("Year", "1985", false));
        list.add(new ItemAttribute("Genre", "Rock", false));
        list.add(new ItemAttribute("Rating", "****", false));
        item.putAttributes(list);

    } catch (SDBException ex) {
        System.out.println(ex.getMessage());
    }
```

Importing the sample data with PHP

First we create the songs domain, then bulk load the 10 items with the
batchPutAttributes function.

```
$sdb = new SimpleDB(awsAccessKey, awsSecretKey);
    // create connection

$domain = "songs";

if($sdb->createDomain($domain)) {
    echo "Domain $domain created<p>";
    echo("RequestId: ".$sdb->RequestId."<br>");
    echo("BoxUsage: ".$sdb->BoxUsage."<p>");

    // build array of items and attribute/value pairs
    $putAttributesRequest = array();

    $item_name = "112222222";
    $putAttributesRequest["Song"] = array("value" => "My Way");
    $putAttributesRequest["Artist"] =
        array("value" => "Frank Sinatra");
    $putAttributesRequest["Year"] = array("value" => "2002");
    $putAttributesRequest["Genre"] =
        array("value" => "Easy Listening");
    $putAttributesRequest["Rating"] =
        array("value" => array("****", "4 stars", "Excellent"));
    $bulkAttr[$item_name] =
        array("name" => "$item_name",
              "attributes" => $putAttributesRequest);

    $item_name = "089997979";
    $putAttributesRequest["Song"] =
        array("value" => "Hotel California");
    $putAttributesRequest["Artist"] =
        array("value" => "Gipsy Kings");
    unset($putAttributesRequest["Year"]);
```

```php
$putAttributesRequest["Genre"] = array("value" => "World");
$putAttributesRequest["Rating"] = array("value" => "****");
$bulkAttr[$item_name] = array("name" => "$item_name",
    "attributes" => $putAttributesRequest);

$item_name = "982411114";
$putAttributesRequest["Song"] = array("value" => "Geraldine");
$putAttributesRequest["Artist"] = array("value" => "Glasvegas");
$putAttributesRequest["Year"] = array("value" => "2008");
$putAttributesRequest["Genre"] =
    array("value" => array("Rock", "Alternative"));
$putAttributesRequest["Rating"] = array("value" => "****");
$bulkAttr[$item_name] = array("name" => "$item_name",
    "attributes" => $putAttributesRequest);

$item_name = "6767969119";
$putAttributesRequest["Song"] = array("value" => "Transmission");
$putAttributesRequest["Artist"] =
    array("value" => "Joy Division");
$putAttributesRequest["Year"] = array("value" => "1981");
$putAttributesRequest["Genre"] = array("value" => "Alternative");
$putAttributesRequest["Rating"] =
    array("value" => array("*****", "Excellent"));
$bulkAttr[$item_name] = array("name" => "$item_name",
    "attributes" => $putAttributesRequest);

$item_name = "6721309888";
$putAttributesRequest["Song"] = array("value" => "Guzarish");
$putAttributesRequest["Artist"] = array("value" => "Ghazini");
$putAttributesRequest["Year"] = array("value" => "2008");
$putAttributesRequest["Genre"] = array("value" => "Bollywood");
$putAttributesRequest["Rating"] =
    array("value" => array("Not rated", "Awful"));
$bulkAttr[$item_name] = array("name" => "$item_name",
    "attributes" => $putAttributesRequest);

$item_name = "0923424244";
$putAttributesRequest["Song"] = array("value" => "So What");
$putAttributesRequest["Artist"] =
    array("value" => "Miles Davis");
$putAttributesRequest["Year"] = array("value" => "1959");
$putAttributesRequest["Genre"] = array("value" => "Jazz");
$putAttributesRequest["Rating"] =
    array("value" => array("*****", "Wow!"));
$bulkAttr[$item_name] = array("name" => "$item_name",
    "attributes" => $putAttributesRequest);

$item_name = "5697878778";
```

```php
$putAttributesRequest["Song"] = array("value" => "Allison");
$putAttributesRequest["Artist"] = array("value" => "Pixies");
$putAttributesRequest["Year"] = array("value" => "1990");
$putAttributesRequest["Genre"] = array("value" => "Alternative");
$putAttributesRequest["Rating"] =
    array("value" => array("****", "4 stars"));
$bulkAttr[$item_name] = array("name" => "$item_name",
    "attributes" => $putAttributesRequest);

$item_name = "7233929292";
$putAttributesRequest["Song"] = array("value" => "Pride");
$putAttributesRequest["Artist"] = array("value" => "Syntax");
unset($putAttributesRequest["Year"]);
$putAttributesRequest["Genre"] =
    array("value" => array("Electronic", "Alternative"));
$putAttributesRequest["Rating"] = array("value" =>
    array("*****", "Excellent"));
$bulkAttr[$item_name] = array("name" => "$item_name",
    "attributes" => $putAttributesRequest);

$item_name = "5656600009";
$putAttributesRequest["Song"] = array("value" => "Acapulco");
$putAttributesRequest["Artist"] =
    array("value" => "Neil Diamond");
$putAttributesRequest["Year"] = array("value" => "1980");
$putAttributesRequest["Genre"] = array("value" => "Soundtrack");
$putAttributesRequest["Rating"] = array("value" =>
    array("*", "1 star", "Avoid"));
$bulkAttr[$item_name] = array("name" => "$item_name",
    "attributes" => $putAttributesRequest);

$item_name = "1002380899";
$putAttributesRequest["Song"] =
    array("value" => "Scream in Blue");
$putAttributesRequest["Artist"] =
    array("value" => "Midnight Oil");
$putAttributesRequest["Year"] = array("value" => "1983");
$putAttributesRequest["Genre"] = array("value" => "Rock");
$putAttributesRequest["Rating"] =
    array("value" => array("***", "3 stars"));
$bulkAttr[$item_name] = array("name" => "$item_name",
    "attributes" => $putAttributesRequest);

$item_name = "1045845425";
$putAttributesRequest["Song"] =
    array("value" => "You're a Strange Animal");
$putAttributesRequest["Artist"] = array("value" => "Gowan");
```

```
    $putAttributesRequest["Year"] = array("value" => "1985");
    $putAttributesRequest["Genre"] = array("value" => "Rock");
    $putAttributesRequest["Rating"] = array("value" => "****");
    $bulkAttr[$item_name] = array("name" => "$item_name",
        "attributes" => $putAttributesRequest);
    echo "batchPutAttributes()<br>";
// batch put the appributes
    if ($sdb->batchPutAttributes($domain,$bulkAttr)) {
        echo("Records created<br>");
        echo("RequestId: ".$sdb->RequestId."<br>");
        echo("BoxUsage: ".$sdb->BoxUsage."<p>");
    } else {
    echo("Records FAILED<br>");
    echo("ErrorCode: ".$sdb->ErrorCode."<p>");
    }
} else {
    echo "Domain $domain create FAILED<p>";
    echo("ErrorCde: ".$sdb->ErrorCode."<p>");
}
```

Details on batchPutAttributes can be found in *Chapter 10, Parallel Processing*.

Importing the sample data with Python

We are going to use the Python console once again to accomplish this task. You can type the commands shown below into a Python console session.

We will first create the domain named songs.

```
>>>
>>>import boto
>>>sdb_connection = boto.connect_sdb()
>>>
>>>songs = sdb_connection.create_domain('songs')
>>>
>>>songs_domain = sdb_connection.get_domain('songs')
>>>
>>>print songs_domain.name
songs
>>>
```

Now that we have the domain, we will import the data into the domain as items.

```
>>>songs_domain.put_attributes('112222222', {'Song':'My
Way', 'Artist':'Frank Sinatra','Year':'2002','Genre':'Easy
Listening','Rating':['****','4 stars','Excellent']})

>>>songs_domain.put_attributes('089997979', {'Song':'Hotel California',
'Artist':'Gipsy Kings','Genre':'World','Rating':'****'})

>>>songs_domain.put_attributes('982411114',{'Song':'Geraldine','Art
ist':'Glasvegas','Year':'2008','Genre':['Rock','Alternative'],'Rati
ng':'*****'})

>>>songs_domain.put_attributes('6767969119',{'Song':'Transmission','Artis
t':'Joy Division','Year':'1981','Genre':'Alternative','Rating':['*****','
Excellent']})

>>>songs_domain.put_attributes('6721309888',{'Song':'Guzarish','A
rtist':'Ghazini','Year':'2008','Genre':'Bollywood','Rating':['Not
rated','Awful']})

>>>songs_domain.put_attributes('0923424244',{'Song':'So
What','Artist':'Miles Davis','Year':'1959','Genre':'Jazz','Rating':['****
*','Wow!']})

>>>songs_domain.put_attributes('5697878778',{'Song':'Allison','Artist':'P
ixies','Year':'1990','Genre':'Alternative','Rating':['****','4 stars']})

>>>songs_domain.put_attributes('7233929292',{'Song':'Pride','Artist':'
Syntax','Genre':['Electronic','Alternative'],'Rating':['*****','Excelle
nt']})

>>>songs_domain.put_attributes('5656600009',{'Song':'Acapulco','Artis
t':'Neil Diamond','Year':'1980','Genre':'Soundtrack','Rating':['*','1
star','Avoid']})

>>>songs_domain.put_attributes('1002380899',{'Song':'Scream in
Blue','Artist':'Midnight Oil','Year':'1983','Genre':'Rock','Rati
ng':['***','3 stars']})

>>>songs_domain.put_attributes('1045845425',{'Song':"You're a Strange Ani
mal",'Artist':'Gowan','Year':'1985','Genre':'Rock','Rating':'****'})
```

We now have a sample dataset imported into SimpleDB and are ready to start exploring the query functionality provided by SimpleDB by running queries and experimenting with this data.

Using Select

SimpleDB supports a **Select** query syntax similar to the one supported by the familiar SQL database queries. This makes it quite easy to get comfortable using it for querying your data.

 The earlier version of SimpleDB supported a different syntax named **Query**, which has since been deprecated in favor of the new Select.

The structure of a Select query is quite simple and is formulated in the following way:

```
SELECT output_list
FROM domain_name
[WHERE expression]
[sort_instructions]
[LIMIT limit]
```

Where:

The `output_list` can be any one of the following:

- `*`: A wildcard that refers to all of the attributes.
- `itemName()`: Only the item name.
- `count(*)`: Only the count.
- An explicit list of attributes (`attribute1,..., attributeN`).

The `domain_name` is the name of the domain to be searched.

The `expression` is the match that you are seeking in your search. This is optional in your query. It can be any of the following:

```
<select expression> intersection <select expression>

NOT <select expression>

(<select expression>)

<select expression> or <select expression>

<select expression> and <select expression>

<simple comparison>
```

The `sort_instructions` describe how to sort the results. This is optional in your query.

The `limit` is the maximum number of results to be returned by the query. The default number of results returned is 100, and the maximum number of results that can be returned in any one query is 2,500. This is optional in your query.

 The total size of the response cannot exceed 1 MB. Amazon SimpleDB automatically adjusts the number of items returned per page to enforce this limit. For example, even if you ask to retrieve 2,500 items, but each individual item is 10 KB in size, the system returns 100 items and an appropriate next token so you can get the next page of results.

Simple select with Java

Let us now run a query against the `songs` domain to retrieve all the song items and their attributes using **Typica**.

```java
SimpleDB sdb = new SimpleDB(awsAccessId, awsSecretKey, true);
try {
    Domain domain = sdb.getDomain("songs");
    String queryString = "SELECT * FROM `songs`";
    int itemCount = 0;
    String nextToken = null;
    do {
        QueryWithAttributesResult queryResults = domain.
selectItems(queryString, nextToken);
        Map<String, List<ItemAttribute>> items = queryResults.
getItems();
        for (String id : items.keySet()) {
            System.out.println("Item : " + id);
            for (ItemAttribute attr : items.get(id)) {
                System.out.println(attr.getName() + " = " + attr.
getValue());
            }
            itemCount++;
        }
        nextToken = queryResults.getNextToken();
    } while (nextToken != null && !nextToken.trim().equals(""));
} catch (SDBException ex) {
    System.out.println(ex.getMessage());
}
```

Simple select with PHP

In the cars domain, we used a simple print_r command. In this sample, we will parse the array. We use a simple Select query (SELECT * FROM songs) against the songs domain. In a later example, we will parse the data.

```php
if (!class_exists('SimpleDB')) require_once('sdb.php');

$sdb = new SimpleDB(awsAccessKey, awsSecretKey); // create connection

$domain = "songs";

$rest = $sdb->select($domain,"select * from $domain");
  // Show all recs
if ($rest) {
    echo "<b>select (all)</b><pre>";
    foreach ($rest as $item) {  // split up items
        echo("Item: ".$item["Name"]."<br>");
        foreach ($item["Attributes"] as $attribute => $value) {
    // split up attributes
      if (is_array($value)) {
        foreach($value as $onevalue) {  // if array of values
          echo("   $attribute = $onevalue<br>");
        }
      } else {  // if single value
        echo("   $attribute = $value<br>");
      }
    }
    echo("<br>");
  }
  echo "</pre><P>";
  echo("RequestId: ".$sdb->RequestId."<br>");
  echo("BoxUsage: ".$sdb->BoxUsage."<br>");
  echo("NextToken: ".$sdb->NextToken."<br>");
} else {
  echo("Listing FAILED<br>");
  echo("ErrorCode: ".$sdb->ErrorCode."<p>");
}
```

This program returns:

```
Item: 089997979
     Song = Hotel California
     Rating = ****
     Genre = World
     Artist = Gipsy Kings

Item: 0923424244
     Year = 1959
     Song = So What
     Rating = *****
     Rating = Wow!
     Genre = Jazz
     Artist = Miles Davis

Item: 1002380899
     Year = 1983
     Song = Scream in Blue
     Rating = ***
     Rating = 3 stars
     Genre = Rock
     Artist = Midnight Oil

Item: 1045845425
     Year = 1985
     Song = You're a Strange
Animal
     Rating = ****
     Genre = Rock
     Artist = Gowan

Item: 112222222
     Year = 2002
     Song = My Way
     Rating = Excellent
     Rating = 4 stars
     Rating = ****
     Genre = Easy Listening
     Artist = Frank Sinatra

Item: 5656600009
     Year = 1980
     Song = Acapulco
     Rating = 1 star
     Rating = Avoid
     Rating = *
     Genre = Soundtrack
     Artist = Neil Diamond
```

```
Item: 5697878778
     Year = 1990
     Song = Allison
     Rating = ****
     Rating = 4 stars
     Genre = Alternative
     Artist = Pixies

Item: 6721309888
     Year = 2008
     Song = Guzarish
     Rating = Not rated
     Rating = Awful
     Genre = Bollywood
     Artist = Ghazini

Item: 6767969119
     Year = 1981
     Song = Transmission
     Rating = *****
     Rating = Excellent
     Genre = Alternative
     Artist = Joy Division

Item: 7233929292
     Song = Pride
     Rating = Excellent
     Rating = *****
     Genre = Electronic
     Genre = Alternative
     Artist = Syntax

Item: 982411114
     Year = 2008
     Song = Geraldine
     Rating = ****
     Genre = Rock
     Genre = Alternative
     Artist = Glasvegas
```

The results are placed here in columns for readability but the actual output is just one long list.

Simple select with Python

Now let's run a simple Select query (SELECT * FROM songs) against the songs domain to retrieve all its items and their attributes.

```
>>>
>>>for item in songs_domain.select("SELECT * FROM `songs`"):
...        print ">>",item.name,item
...
>> 112222222 {u'Genre': u'Easy Listening', u'Rating': [u'****',
u'Excellent', u'4 stars'], u'Year': u'2002', u'Artist': u'Frank Sinatra',
u'Song': u'My Way'}

>> 089997979 {u'Genre': u'World', u'Rating': u'****', u'Song': u'Hotel
California', u'Artist': u'Gipsy Kings'}

>> 982411114 {u'Genre': [u'Rock', u'Alternative'], u'Rating': u'*****',
u'Year': u'2008', u'Artist':
u'Glasvegas', u'Song': u'Geraldine'}

>> 6767969119 {u'Genre': u'Alternative', u'Rating': [u'Excellent',
u'*****'], u'Year': u'1981', u'Artist': u'Joy Division', u'Song':
u'Transmission'}

>> 6721309888 {u'Genre': u'Bollywood', u'Rating': [u'Not rated',
u'Awful'], u'Year': u'2008', u'Artist': u'Ghazini', u'Song': u'Guzarish'}

>> 0923424244 {u'Genre': u'Jazz', u'Rating': [u'*****', u'Wow!'],
u'Year': u'1959', u'Artist': u'Miles Davis', u'Song': u'So What'}

>> 5697878778 {u'Genre': u'Alternative', u'Rating': [u'4 stars',
u'****'], u'Year': u'1990', u'Artist': u'Pixies', u'Song': u'Allison'}

>> 7233929292 {u'Genre': [u'Alternative', u'Electronic'], u'Rating':
[u'Excellent', u'*****'], u'Song': u'Pride', u'Artist': u'Syntax'}

>> 5656600009 {u'Genre': u'Soundtrack', u'Rating': [u'1 star', u'*',
u'Avoid'], u'Year': u'1980', u'Artist': u'Neil Diamond', u'Song':
u'Acapulco'}

>> 1002380899 {u'Genre': u'Rock', u'Rating': [u'***', u'3 stars'],
u'Year': u'1983', u'Artist': u'Midnight Oil', u'Song': u'Scream in Blue'}

>>>
```

Quoting values in Select expressions

All attribute values inside a `selectexpression` must be quoted with either a single or double quote. If the attribute value itself contains a quote, you must escape it with the same quote symbol. If you have a single quote as a part of the value, you need to escape it like this:

```
select * from mydomain where attr1 = '"That''s wonderful!"'
```

You can also use a double quote for escaping like this:

```
select * from mydomain where attr1 = """That's wonderful!"""
```

> If the name of the domain or attribute contains characters other than only letters, numbers, underscores (_), or dollar symbols ($), you must escape the name with a backtick character (`). This makes using characters like the dash (-) more complex. When a domain or attribute name has a dash, you create the domain and the attributes without the backtick.
>
> The backtick is required for the SELECT operation ONLY. The PHP samples use the domain name car-s to illustrate this.

```
select * from `my-domain` where `timestamp-1` > '1194393600'
```

If a backtick is part of the name for the domain or attribute, it must be escaped by using two backticks. There is also a set of SimpleDB reserved keywords that must be escaped by using backticks if you are using them as a part of the name for a domain or an attribute. The backticks are required only if the keyword constitutes the entire name, and not just a part of the name.

Here is the list of the reserved keywords:

- or
- and
- not
- from
- where
- select
- like
- null
- is
- order

- by
- asc
- desc
- in
- between
- intersection
- limit
- every

Predicates in Select expressions

A SimpleDB query **predicate** is the expression that specifies your search criteria by comparing the value of an attribute with a constant value. Each predicate uses comparison operators for specifying the search criteria in the **Select** expression.

Simple predicate query with Java

For instance, a **predicate** that matches all songs released in the year 1980 in our songs domain would look like this in Java:

```java
SimpleDB sdb = new SimpleDB(awsAccessId, awsSecretKey, true);
try {
    Domain domain = sdb.getDomain("songs");
    String queryString = "SELECT * FROM `songs`
        WHERE `Year` = '1980'";
    int itemCount = 0;
    String nextToken = null;
    do {
        QueryWithAttributesResult queryResults = domain
            .selectItems(queryString, nextToken);
        Map<String, List<ItemAttribute>> items = queryResults
            .getItems();
        for (String id : items.keySet()) {
            System.out.println("Item : " + id);
            for (ItemAttribute attr : items.get(id)) {
                System.out.println("      " + attr.getName() + " = "
                + attr.getValue());
            }
            itemCount++;
        }
        nextToken = queryResults.getNextToken();
    } while (nextToken != null && !nextToken.trim().equals(""));
```

```
} catch (SDBException ex) {
    System.out.println(ex.getMessage());
}
```

Simple predicate query with PHP

The following program is the same as the previous with the exception of the revised SQL:

```php
if (!class_exists('SimpleDB')) require_once('sdb.php');
$sdb = new SimpleDB(awsAccessKey, awsSecretKey);
// create connection
$domain = "songs";
$rest = $sdb->select($domain,"select * from $domain
    where Year = '1980'");
if ($rest) {
    echo "<b>select (all)</b><pre>";
    foreach ($rest as $item) {  // split up items
        echo("Item: ".$item["Name"]."<br>");
        foreach ($item["Attributes"] as $attribute => $value)
        { // split up attributes
            if (is_array($value)) {
                foreach($value as $onevalue) {  // if array of values
                    echo("   
                        $attribute = $onevalue<br>");
                }
            } else {  // if single value
            echo("   $attribute = $value<br>");
            }
        }
        echo("<br>");
    }
    echo "</pre><P>";
    echo("RequestId: ".$sdb->RequestId."<br>");
    echo("BoxUsage: ".$sdb->BoxUsage."<br>");
    echo("NextToken: ".$sdb->NextToken."<br>");
} else {
    echo("Listing FAILED<br>");
    echo("ErrorCode: ".$sdb->ErrorCode."<p>");
}
}
```

This program returns:

```
Item: 1045845425
    Year = 1985
    Song = You're a Strange Animal
    Rating = ****
    Genre = Rock
    Artist = Gowan
```

Simple predicate query with Python

Here is the same query using Python:

```
>>>for item in songs_domain.select("SELECT * FROM `songs` WHERE `Year` =
'1980'"):
...       print ">>",item.name,item
...
>> 5656600009 {u'Genre': u'Soundtrack', u'Rating': [u'1 star', u'*',
u'Avoid'], u'Year': u'1980', u'Artist': u'Neil Diamond', u'Song':
u'Acapulco'}

>>>
```

We will discuss all the comparison operators that are currently supported by SimpleDB for use in your **Select** expressions in the next section.

Comparison operators

Comparison operators are applied to a single attribute in your query expressions and are lexicographical in nature. We looked in detail at lexicographical comparisons and different methods for storing data in SimpleDB to make comparisons between attribute values easier in the *Chapter 5, Data Types*.

The various comparison operators that are currently supported by SimpleDB are:

=	Attribute value or `itemName()` equals the specified constant.
!=	Attribute value or `itemName()` does not equal the specified constant.
>	Attribute value or `itemName()` is greater than the specified constant.
>=	Attribute value or `itemName()` is greater than or equal to the specified constant.
<	Attribute value or `itemName()` is less than the specified constant.
<=	Attribute value or `itemName()` is less than or equal to the specified constant.

like	Attribute value or itemName() contains the specified constant. The like operator can be used to evaluate the start of a string (string%), the end of a string (%string), or any part of a string ('%string%'). This operator is case-sensitive.
not like	Attribute value or itemName() does not contain the specified constant. The not like operator can be used to evaluate the start of a string (string%), the end of a string (%string), or any part of a string (%string%).
between	Attribute value or itemName() falls within a range, including the start and end value.
in	Attribute value or itemName() is equal to one of the specified constants. When used with items, it acts as a batch get.
is null	Attribute does not exist. If an item has the attribute with an empty string, it is not returned.
is not null	Attribute value or itemName() contains any value.
every()	For multi-valued attributes, every attribute value must satisfy the constraint.

The maximum number of comparisons that you can use in a single Select expression is 20. Also, the maximum number of constants used with the **in** keyword is 20.

In the next section, we will be using these comparison operators in our sample queries against the sample songs data. The only difference with the simple query programs discussed is to change the SQL line.

Queries with Select

Now let us run some simple queries against the data that we imported into the songs domain and get familiar with the syntax. Using one of the three examples discussed, you can create the songs domain in your SimpleDB database. Using either the SDBtool Firefox plugin that was discussed in *Chapter 2, Getting Started with SimpleDB*, or the PHP Try-SQL-Queries sample program, you can try these SQL queries as well as variations on them.

Comparison operators

Select all attribute/values from songs where the Song attribute is My Way. It is important to note that domains and attributes are case-sensitive.

Enter:

```
SELECT * FROM songs WHERE Song = 'My Way'
```

Result:

Item name	Song	Artist	Year	Genre	Rating
112222222	My Way	Frank Sinatra	2002	Easy Listening	**** 4 stars Excellent

The list of available comparison operators includes =, !=, >, >=, <, and <=.

Greater than

Retrieve all songs where the Year is greater than 2000.

 In *Chapter 4, The SimpleDB Data Model*, we discussed how all data in SimpleDB is stored in UTF-8 strings. In the sample songs domain, the Year is normalized to four characters, so this query works. For more details on numeric normalization, see *Chapter 5, Data Types*.

Enter:

```
SELECT * FROM songs WHERE Year > '2000'
```

Result:

Item name	Song	Artist	Year	Genre	Rating
112222222	My Way	Frank Sinatra	2002	Easy Listening	**** 4 stars Excellent
982411114	Geraldine	Glasvegas	2008	Rock Alternative	******
6721309888	Guzarish	Ghazini	2008	Bollywood	Not rated Awful

In the sample `songs` domain, the `Year` is normalized to four characters, so this query works as expected. No data normalization was needed as the data was normalized by its default structure and range.

LIKE

Retrieve all songs in our dataset that are rated either three stars or higher than three stars (***):

Enter:

```
SELECT * FROM songs WHERE Rating LIKE '***%'
```

The `LIKE` command is a substring query into a value. The % is the wildcard, so in this example, we want items that begin with ***.

Result:

Item name	Song	Artist	Year	Genre	Rating
112222222	My Way	Frank Sinatra	2002	Easy Listening	**** 4 stars Excellent
089997979	Hotel California	Gipsy Kings		World	****
982411114	Geraldine	Glasvegas	2008	Rock Alternative	*****
6767969119	Transmission	Joy Division	1981	Alternative	***** Excellent
0923424244	So What	Miles Davis	1959	Jazz	***** Wow!
5697878778	Allison	Pixies	1990	Alternative	**** 4 stars
7233929292	Pride	Syntax		Electronic Alternative	***** Excellent
1002380899	Scream in Blue	Midnight Oil	1983	Rock	*** 3 stars
1045845425	You're a Strange Animal	Gowan	1985	Rock	****

A variation in the last SQL is:

Enter:

```
SELECT * FROM songs WHERE Rating LIKE '%stars'
```

Result:

Item name	Song	Artist	Year	Genre	Rating
112222222	My Way	Frank Sinatra	2002	Easy Listening	**** 4 stars Excellent
5697878778	Allison	Pixies	1990	Alternative	**** 4 stars
1002380899	Scream in Blue	Midnight Oil	1983	Rock	*** 3 stars

While this looks like a similar statement, it is very different from a performance perspective. The LIKE '***%' command is looking for a value beginning with *** while the LIKE '%stars' command is looking for a value ending with stars. While the functionality is almost identical, the performance can be dramatically different. Looking for what a value begins with can be done in the index; looking for what a value ends with forces a full table scan. The % wild_card can be put on both ends, such as '%star%' finding any item where the word star is somewhere in the value. Putting % on both ends also forces a full table scan, as each value is individually compared to see if star is in the string.

NOT LIKE

Retrieve all songs in our dataset whose genre does not begin with 'Jazz'

Enter:

```
SELECT * FROM songs WHERE Genre NOT LIKE 'Jazz%'
```

This query puts a NOT in front of the LIKE to give us select items where the Genre does not begin with Jazz.

Result:

Item name	Song	Artist	Year	Genre	Rating
112222222	My Way	Frank Sinatra	2002	Easy Listening	**** 4 stars Excellent
089997979	Hotel California	Gipsy Kings		World	****
982411114	Geraldine	Glasvegas	2008	Rock Alternative	*****
6767969119	Transmission	Joy Division	1981	Alternative	***** Excellent
6721309888	Guzarish	Ghazini	2008	Bollywood	Not rated Awful
5697878778	Allison	Pixies	1990	Alternative	**** 4 stars
7233929292	Pride	Syntax		Electronic Alternative	***** Excellent
5656600009	Acapulco	Neil Diamond	1980	Soundtrack	* 1 star Avoid
1002380899	Scream in Blue	Midnight Oil	1983	Rock	*** 3 stars
1045845425	You're a Strange Animal	Gowan	1985	Rock	****

BETWEEN

Retrieve all songs that were released between the years 1980 and 2000:

Enter:

```
SELECT * FROM songs WHERE Year BETWEEN '1980' AND '2000'
```

Or enter:

```
SELECT * FROM songs WHERE Year >= '1980' AND Year <= '2000'
```

Both return the same records and use the same box usage.

Item name	Song	Artist	Year	Genre	Rating
6767969119	Transmission	Joy Division	1981	Alternative	***** Excellent
5697878778	Allison	Pixies	1990	Alternative	**** 4 stars
5656600009	Acapulco	Neil Diamond	1980	Soundtrack	* 1 star Avoid
1002380899	Scream in Blue	Midnight Oil	1983	Rock	*** 3 stars
1045845425	You're a Strange Animal	Gowan	1985	Rock	****

IN

Retrieve all songs that were released in one of the years 1980, 1990, or 2008:

Enter:

```
SELECT * FROM songs WHERE Year IN ('1980','1990','2008')
```

The maximum number of constants in the IN statement is 20. Using IN is much cleaner than using:

```
SELECT * FROM songs WHERE Year='1980' OR Year='1990' OR Year='2008'
```

Result:

Item name	Song	Artist	Year	Genre	Rating
982411114	Geraldine	Glasvegas	2008	Rock Alternative	*****
6721309888	Guzarish	Ghazini	2008	Bollywood	Not rated Awful
5697878778	Allison	Pixies	1990	Alternative	**** 4 stars
5656600009	Acapulco	Neil Diamond	1980	Soundtrack	* 1 star Avoid

IS NULL

Retrieve all the songs without a release year:

Enter:

```
SELECT * FROM songs WHERE Year IS NULL
```

Result:

Item name	Song	Artist	Year	Genre	Rating
089997979	Hotel California	Gipsy Kings		World	****
7233929292	Pride	Syntax		Electronic Alternative	***** Excellent

IS NULL is NOT the same as ="

If you want to check for items where there is no value for an attribute, you must use IS NULL.

IS NOT NULL

Retrieve all the songs with a release year:

Enter:

```
SELECT * FROM songs WHERE Year IS NOT NULL
```

Result:

Item name	Song	Artist	Year	Genre	Rating
112222222	My Way	Frank Sinatra	2002	Easy Listening	**** 4 stars Excellent
982411114	Geraldine	Glasvegas	2008	Rock Alternative	*****
6767969119	Transmission	Joy Division	1981	Alternative	***** Excellent
6721309888	Guzarish	Ghazini	2008	Bollywood	Not rated Awful
0923424244	So What	Miles Davis	1959	Jazz	***** Wow!

Item name	Song	Artist	Year	Genre	Rating
5697878778	Allison	Pixies	1990	Alternative	**** 4 stars
5656600009	Acapulco	Neil Diamond	1980	Soundtrack	* 1 star Avoid
1002380899	Scream in Blue	Midnight Oil	1983	Rock	*** 3 stars
1045845425	You're a Strange Animal	Gowan	1985	Rock	****

The other use of IS NOT NULL is with ORDER BY.

EVERY()

The `rating` attribute in our dataset can have multiple values—ratings with just stars, a rating such as 4 stars, and a rating blurb or comment. Select with `Ratings='****'` will find all items with a rating of `'****'` as well as items with other ratings. `EVERY()` is used to retrieve all items which ONLY have one rating value—`'****'`.

Enter:

```
SELECT * FROM songs WHERE Rating = '****'
```

Returns:

Item name	Song	Artist	Year	Genre	Rating
112222222	My Way	Frank Sinatra	2002	Easy Listening	**** 4 stars Excellent
089997979	Hotel California	Gipsy Kings		World	****
982411114	Geraldine	Glasvegas	2008	Rock Alternative	*****
6767969119	Transmission	Joy Division	1981	Alternative	***** Excellent
6721309888	Guzarish	Ghazini	2008	Bollywood	Not rated Awful
0923424244	So What	Miles Davis	1959	Jazz	***** Wow!
5697878778	Allison	Pixies	1990	Alternative	**** 4 stars

Item name	Song	Artist	Year	Genre	Rating
1045845425	You're a Strange Animal	Gowan	1985	Rock	****

Not putting in EVERY returns all items where one of the rating values is '****'.

Each attribute in an item is considered individually against the comparison conditions defined by you in the predicate. Item names are selected if any of the values match the predicate condition. To change this behavior, you must use the every() operator to return results where every attribute matches the query expression.

Now enter:

```
SELECT * FROM songs WHERE EVERY(Rating) = '****'
```

To return:

Item name	Song	Artist	Year	Genre	Rating
089997979	Hotel California	Gipsy Kings		World	****
1045845425	You're a Strange Animal	Gowan	1985	Rock	****

EVERY in the SQL requires that all rating values are '****'. The My Way record is not returned, as it has three rating values and all are not '****'.

Combining expressions

Multiple select expressions can be combined using: INTERSECTION, OR, AND, NOT, and parentheses ( ).

```
<select expression> intersection <select expression>
```

```
NOT <select expression>
```

```
(<select expression>)
```

```
<select expression> or <select expression>
```

```
<select expression> and <select expression>
```

SimpleDB supports both the set operators—INTERSECTION and UNION. The INTERSECTION operator can be used to retrieve items matching the specified predicates on both sides of the operator. The UNION operator is used for retrieving items that match either of the specified predicates. The UNION operator works only with the old query syntax and will not work with the new Select syntax. You should use the OR operator instead of UNION.

INTERSECTION

Retrieve all songs that are released after 1980 and are in the Rock genre:

```
SELECT * FROM songs WHERE Year > '1980' INTERSECTION Genre = 'Rock'
```

`SELECT * FROM songs WHERE Year > '1980'` returns:

Item name	Song	Artist	Year	Genre	Rating
112222222	My Way	Frank Sinatra	2002	Easy Listening	**** 4 stars Excellent
982411114	Geraldine	Glasvegas	2008	Rock Alternative	*****
6767969119	Transmission	Joy Division	1981	Alternative	***** Excellent
6721309888	Guzarish	Ghazini	2008	Bollywood	Not rated Awful
5697878778	Allison	Pixies	1990	Alternative	**** 4 stars
1002380899	Scream in Blue	Midnight Oil	1983	Rock	*** 3 stars
1045845425	You're a Strange Animal	Gowan	1985	Rock	****

`SELECT * FROM songs WHERE Genre = 'Rock'` returns:

Item name	Song	Artist	Year	Genre	Rating
982411114	Geraldine	Glasvegas	2008	Rock Alternative	*****
1002380899	Scream in Blue	Midnight Oil	1983	Rock	*** 3 stars
1045845425	You're a Strange Animal	Gowan	1985	Rock	****

The common items are highlighted and are what would be returned for the INTERSECTION.

The result is the same for:

`SELECT * FROM songs WHERE Year > '1980' AND Genre = 'Rock'`

NOT

You can negate the search query by using the Not Boolean operator. Here is how you can retrieve all songs that are not released before 1980 and are not in the 'Rock' genre:

`SELECT * FROM songs WHERE NOT Year < '1980' INTERSECTION NOT Genre = 'Rock'`

`SELECT * FROM songs WHERE NOT Year < '1980'` returns:

Item name	Song	Artist	Year	Genre	Rating
112222222	My Way	Frank Sinatra	2002	Easy Listening	**** 4 stars Excellent
982411114	Geraldine	Glasvegas	2008	Rock Alternative	*****
6767969119	Transmission	Joy Division	1981	Alternative	***** Excellent
6721309888	Guzarish	Ghazini	2008	Bollywood	Not rated Awful
5697878778	Allison	Pixies	1990	Alternative	**** 4 stars

Item name	Song	Artist	Year	Genre	Rating
5656600009	Acapulco	Neil Diamond	1980	Soundtrack	* 1 star Avoid
1002380899	Scream in Blue	Midnight Oil	1983	Rock	*** 3 stars
1045845425	You're a Strange Animal	Gowan	1985	Rock	****

`SELECT * FROM songs WHERE NOT Genre = 'Rock'` returns:

Item name	Song	Artist	Year	Genre	Rating
112222222	My Way	Frank Sinatra	2002	Easy Listening	**** 4 stars Excellent
089997979	Hotel California	Gipsy Kings		World	****
982411114	Geraldine	Glasvegas	2008	Rock Alternative	*****
6767969119	Transmission	Joy Division	1981	Alternative	***** Excellent
6721309888	Guzarish	Ghazini	2008	Bollywood	Not rated Awful
0923424244	So What	Miles Davis	1959	Jazz	***** Wow!
5697878778	Allison	Pixies	1990	Alternative	**** 4 stars
7233929292	Pride	Syntax		Electronic Alternative	***** Excellent
5656600009	Acapulco	Neil Diamond	1980	Soundtrack	* 1 star Avoid

The `INTERSECTION` items are highlighted.

 SimpleDB evaluates all the predicates and set operators that are part of the Select query in order from left to right. If you use a not operator, it will be applied to the first set operator that it precedes in the expression.

OR

SimpleDB suggests that you use the OR operator instead of using the **union** operator, which is only for working with the old query syntax. Here is how we can retrieve all songs that either have a rating of ★★★★ stars or are released after 1980:

```
SELECT * FROM songs WHERE Year > '1980' OR Rating = '****'
```

Returns:

Item name	Song	Artist	Year	Genre	Rating
112222222	My Way	Frank Sinatra	2002	Easy Listening	**** 4 stars Excellent
089997979	Hotel California	Gipsy Kings		World	****
982411114	Geraldine	Glasvegas	2008	Rock Alternative	*****
6767969119	Transmission	Joy Division	1981	Alternative	***** Excellent
6721309888	Guzarish	Ghazini	2008	Bollywood	Not rated Awful
0923424244	So What	Miles Davis	1959	Jazz	***** Wow!
5697878778	Allison	Pixies	1990	Alternative	**** 4 stars
7233929292	Pride	Syntax		Electronic Alternative	***** Excellent
5656600009	Acapulco	Neil Diamond	1980	Soundtrack	* 1 star Avoid
1002380899	Scream in Blue	Midnight Oil	1983	Rock	*** 3 stars
1045845425	You're a Strange Animal	Gowan	1985	Rock	****

OR Rating='****' adds the 'Hotel California' items to the returned items from Year > '1980'.

Sorting

SimpleDB supports sorting your query results, but please keep in mind that all comparisons of attributes and values are done in the lexicographical fashion that we discussed in the previous chapter. All data that you intend to sort that is not a plain string, but is a date or a number or a Boolean, must be appropriately encoded when storing it and then decoded correctly on retrieval. You can sort data based on a single attribute or the item names, in either ascending or descending order. If you do not specify a sort order, the results are sorted in the ascending order by default. Sorting is done by specifying the keywords order by and either asc or desc in the expression.

SimpleDB provides the following guidelines that you must be aware of when sorting the data:

- All sort operations are of course performed in lexicographical order
- If you want to sort your results, you must provide the sort attribute in at least one of the predicates of the expression
- You can apply sorting to expressions that contain the is null predicate operator, as long as is null is not applied to the attribute on which you are sorting

Retrieve all songs released before 2000 and list them in the ascending order:

```
SELECT * FROM songs WHERE Year < '1981' ORDER BY Year ASC
```

Returns:

Item name	Song	Artist	Year	Genre	Rating
0923424244	So What	Miles Davis	1959	Jazz	***** Wow!
6767969119	Transmission	Joy Division	1981	Alternative	***** Excellent

If you do not specify a sorting order, the results will by default be sorted in ascending order, so this SQL gives the same results.

```
SELECT * FROM songs WHERE Year < '1981' ORDER BY Year
```

Let us make the same query, but order the results in a descending order of the year of release:

```
SELECT * FROM songs WHERE Year < '1981' ORDER BY Year DESC
```

Returns:

Item name	Song	Artist	Year	Genre	Rating
6767969119	Transmission	Joy Division	1981	Alternative	***** Excellent
0923424244	So What	Miles Davis	1959	Jazz	***** Wow!

Retrieve all songs released before the year 2000 and sort them in descending order by artist name. We have to specify a predicate for Artist in order to use the sort on the `Artist`.

```
SELECT * FROM songs WHERE Year < '2000' INTERSECTION Artist IS NOT
NULL ORDER BY Artist DESC
```

Results:

Item name	Song	Artist	Year	Genre	Rating
5697878778	Allison	Pixies	1990	Alternative	**** 4 stars
5656600009	Acapulco	Neil Diamond	1980	Soundtrack	* 1 star Avoid
0923424244	So What	Miles Davis	1959	Jazz	***** Wow!
1002380899	Scream in Blue	Midnight Oil	1983	Rock	*** 3 stars
6767969119	Transmission	Joy Division	1981	Alternative	***** Excellent
1045845425	You're a Strange Animal	Gowan	1985	Rock	****

If you use:

```
SELECT * FROM songs WHERE Year < '2000' ORDER BY Artist DESC
```

This will give an `InvalidSortExpression` error, as Artist is not specified as a predicate. This takes a bit of getting used to.

Counting the results

SimpleDB provides a simple way for you to count the number of items in a result set. You can get the number of items only by specifying the keyword `count(*)` in the predicate. There is no restriction on the maximum number of counted results. However, there are certain limits placed by SimpleDB on the query itself:

- The count request must not take more than five seconds. In case it exceeds the five second time limit, SimpleDB will return the number of items that it could count until the timeout, and a next token to return additional results. You will need to use the returned marker token in your next query to request the remaining items.

- Sometimes, your request may time out. If this is the case, SimpleDB will return a 408 error that is a 'Request Timeout'. You will need to resubmit the request.

COUNT()

Retrieve the number of songs in our `songs` domain that were released before 2000:

```
SELECT count(*) FROM songs WHERE Year < '2000'
```

Returns:

```
Item: Domain
  Count = 6
```

Retrieve the number of songs in our `songs` domain and limit it to 3:

```
SELECT count(*) FROM songs LIMIT 3
```

This statement is interesting, as the LIMIT puts a cap on the count. The query will return a count of 3, but also a `NextToken` as there are more results to come.

Queries on multi-valued attributes

One of the unique features of SimpleDB is the ability to associate multiple values with a single attribute. In our songs dataset, the `Rating` and `Genre` attributes for an item can have multiple values. You can store a star-based rating, a string rating, and a comment for the `Rating` attribute. SimpleDB makes it very easy to query for items with multi-valued attributes.

Querying for multi-valued attributes

Retrieve all songs with a rating of 4 stars or ****:

```
SELECT * FROM songs WHERE Rating = '****' OR Rating = '4 stars'
```

To retrieve all songs with a rating of '4 stars' and '****' use:

```
SELECT * FROM songs WHERE Rating = '****' INTERSECTION
                          Rating = '4 stars'
```

While it may seem logical to use AND, it is not syntactically acceptable to SimpleDB.

getAttribute

SELECT is the most common technique to retrieve items from SimpleDB, but one special case is retrieving one item using the item name. This can be done with a SELECT query, but getAttributes uses about 41% of the box usage of the SELECT query.

getAttributes in Java

In this example, we will retrieve the attributes for an item from SimpleDB. Typica provides a method called getItemsAttributes(), which uses getAttributes under the covers.

```java
SimpleDB sdb = new SimpleDB(awsAccessId, awsSecretKey, true);
try {
    Domain domain = sdb.getDomain("songs");
    List<String> itemsToGet = new ArrayList<String>();
    itemsToGet.add("112222222");
    Map<String, List<ItemAttribute>> items = domain.
getItemsAttributes(itemsToGet);
    for (String id : items.keySet()) {
        System.out.println("Item : " + id);
        for (ItemAttribute attr : items.get(id)) {
            System.out.println("     " + attr.getName() + " = " +
attr.getValue());
        }
    }
} catch (SDBException ex) {
    System.out.println(ex.getMessage());
}
```

getAttributes in PHP

In the following example, we fetch the attributes for the item:

```
$sdb = new SimpleDB(awsAccessKey, awsSecretKey); // create connection
$domain = "songs";
// create connection
$sdb = new SimpleDB(awsAccessKey, awsSecretKey);
$item_name = "112222222";
$rest = $sdb->getAttributes($domain,$item_name);
if ($rest) {
    echo "getAttributes for $item_name<pre>";
    print_r($rest);
    echo "</pre><P>";
    echo("RequestId: ".$sdb->RequestId."<br>");
    echo("BoxUsage: ".$sdb->BoxUsage."<br>");
    echo("NextToken: ".$sdb->NextToken."<br>");
    $getattrbox = $sdb->BoxUsage;
} else {
    echo("Listing FAILED<br>");
    echo("ErrorCode: ".$sdb->ErrorCode."<p>");
}
echo("<p>Versus using:<P>");
$rest = $sdb->select($domain,"select * from $domain WHERE
                    itemName() = '112222222'");
if ($rest) {
    echo "<b>SELECT * FROM SONGS
        WHERE itemName() = '112222222'</b><pre>";
    print_r($rest);
    echo "</pre><P>";
    echo("RequestId: ".$sdb->RequestId."<br>");
    echo("BoxUsage: ".$sdb->BoxUsage."<br>");
    echo("NextToken: ".$sdb->NextToken."<br>");
} else {
    echo("Listing FAILED<br>");
    echo("ErrorCode: ".$sdb->ErrorCode."<p>");
}
```

Result:

```
getAttributes for 112222222
Array
(
   [Year] => 2002
```

```
    [Song] => My Way
    [Rating] => Array
      (
        [0] => ****
        [1] => 4 stars
        [2] => Excellent
      )
    [Genre] => Easy Listening
    [Artist] => Frank Sinatra
)
RequestId: f411b24c-c6ae-8b60-da54-0421bfb51b83
BoxUsage: 0.0000093702
```

Versus using:

```
SELECT * FROM SONGS WHERE itemName() = '112222222'
```

```
Array
(
  [0] => Array
    (
      [Name] => 112222222
      [Attributes] => Array
        (
          [Year] => 2002
          [Song] => My Way
          [Rating] => Array
            (
              [0] => ****
              [1] => Excellent
              [2] => 4 stars
            )
          [Genre] => Easy Listening
          [Artist] => Frank Sinatra
        )
    )
)
RequestId: 21f7fbe1-70d2-e501-1cfd-e3a62b51504c
BoxUsage: 0.0000228616
```

getAttributes in Python

Here is how you can use the `getAttributes` for an item from SimpleDB using Python and **boto**.

```
>>>item = songs_domain.get_attributes("112222222")
>>>print ">>",item.name,item


>> 112222222{u'Genre': u'Easy Listening', u'Rating': [u'****',
u'Excellent', u'4 stars'], u'Year': u'2002', u'Artist': u'Frank Sinatra',
u'Song': u'My Way'}


>>>
```

The data response is different, so the trade-off is the reduced box usage versus the different interface. If your application does a lot of single item reads, the extra coding may be worth it.

Summary

In this chapter, we discussed the Select syntax for retrieving results from SimpleDB. We looked at the various operators and how to create predicates that allow us to get back the information we need. In the next chapter, we are going to look at storing large binary objects in Amazon S3 while using SimpleDB as the metadata store for these objects.

7
Storing Data on S3

In the previous chapter, we stored data about our songs collection on SimpleDB. But where are the actual MP3 files for these songs? They are stored locally on your hard drive. Wouldn't it be nice if we stored those on the cloud too? We cannot store them in SimpleDB, as it is not made for storing large binary files. However, Amazon does provide another web service that is perfect for storing files — the **Amazon Simple Storage Service (S3)**. In this chapter, we are going to learn how to store the metadata about our songs collection on SimpleDB, while storing the actual song files on S3. We will also cover:

- Learn about S3 buckets
- Create an S3 bucket for storing our songs
- Add metadata about the songs to SimpleDB
- Store the actual song files on S3
- Back up SimpleDB domains to S3

Amazon S3

Amazon S3 is a highly scalable and fast Internet data-storage system. It provides a query-based interface and is simple to use. There are three fundamental components that comprise S3 — buckets, objects, and keys. We are going to discuss each of these here.

Buckets

Buckets are the fundamental building blocks in S3. Each object stored in S3 is contained within a bucket. A bucket is quite similar to a directory on the filesystem. The key advantage of an S3 bucket is that the bucket and its contents are addressable using a URL. For example, if you have a bucket named `songs`, with a file `mysong.mp3`, it can be addressed using the URL `http://songs.s3.amazonaws.com/mysong.mp3`.

Each S3 account can contain a maximum of 100 buckets. You can ensure the bucket is situated in a certain geographic location by specifying it at the time the bucket is created. Currently S3 is available in two different regions—the United States and the European Union. Amazon has recently announced that they are expanding to a third geographical region, likely to be in Singapore, in 2010.

S3 enforces certain requirements on the naming of buckets:

- The name must start with a number or a letter.
- The name must be between 3 and 255 characters.
- A valid name can contain only lowercase letters, numbers, periods, underscores, and hyphens.
- Though names can have numbers and periods, they cannot be in the IP address format. You cannot name a bucket 192.168.1.254.
- The bucket namespace is shared among all buckets from all of the accounts in S3. Your bucket name must be unique across the entire S3.

If you intend to use the addressable URLs, the name of your bucket must conform to the following additional requirements:

- The name of the bucket must not contain any underscores.
- The name must be between 3 and 63 characters.
- The name cannot end with a dash or have dashes next to periods in the name. For example, `myfavorite-.bucket.com` is invalid.

Objects

Objects contain the actual data that will be stored in an S3 bucket. In our case, the song MP3 files that we will storing in S3 are the objects. There are no restrictions on the number of objects that can be stored in S3, but a single object cannot be larger than 5 GB in size. As we are only storing song files, we should theoretically not hit this limit!

Keys

Objects that are stored in an S3 bucket are identified using unique keys. This is the name that you provide for the object, and it must of course be unique within the bucket, just as the name of a file must be unique within a directory on your filesystem.

In our case, we can use the name of the song as the key. This might present a slight difficulty as your song collection grows, as the name may no longer be unique. We can add the name of the artist to the song to make it a little bit more unique. A better solution would be to use some kind of a unique key as the object name. We will use a MD5 hash that should be unique enough for our purposes.

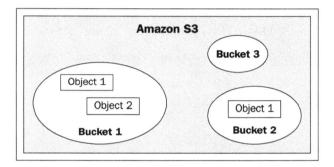

Pricing for S3

The charges for S3 are calculated based upon three criteria which are different based upon the geographic location of your buckets:

- **The total amount of storage space used**: This includes the actual size of your data content and the associated metadata. The unit used by S3 for determining the storage consumed is GB-Month. The number of bytes of storage used by your account is computed every hour, and at the end of the month it is converted into the storage used by you for the month.

Location	Cost
United States	$0.15 per GB-Month of storage used
Europe	$0.18 per GB-Month of storage used

- **The amount of data or bandwidth transferred to and from S3**: This includes all data that is uploaded and downloaded from S3. There is no charge for data transferred between EC2 and S3 buckets that are located in the United States, while data transferred between EC2 and European S3 buckets is charged at the standard data transfer rate as shown following:

Location	Cost
United States	$0.100 per GB—all data transfer in
	$0.170 per GB—first 10 TB / month data transfer out
	$0.130 per GB—next 40 TB / month data transfer out
	$0.110 per GB—next 100 TB / month data transfer out
	$0.100 per GB—data transfer out / month over 150 TB
Europe	$0.100 per GB—all data transfer in
	$0.170 per GB—first 10 TB / month data transfer out
	$0.130 per GB—next 40 TB / month data transfer out
	$0.110 per GB—next 100 TB / month data transfer out
	$0.100 per GB—data transfer out / month over 150 TB

- **The number of API requests performed**: S3 charges fees per each request that is made using the interface—for creating objects, listing buckets, listing objects, and so on. There is no fee for deleting objects and buckets. The fees are once again slightly different based on the geographical location of the bucket. The pricing for API requests is as follows:

Location	Cost
United States	$0.01 per 1,000 PUT, POST, or LIST requests
	$0.01 per 10,000 GET and all other requests
	No charge for delete requests
Europe	$0.012 per 1,000 PUT, POST, or LIST requests
	$0.012 per 10,000 GET and all other requests
	No charge for delete requests

The pricing shown in the above table is current at the time of writing this chapter, but it is likely that it might have changed since. You can always get the latest pricing for S3 at the Amazon Web Services S3 web page.

Plan of action

We are going to store the metadata for our songs collection on SimpleDB and also store the corresponding MP3 files on S3. The following figure shows what we are going to accomplish:

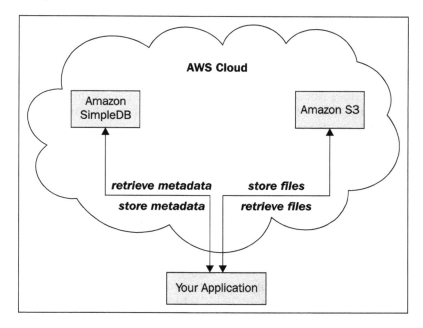

In order to accomplish this, here is the sequence of steps we need to take:

1. Create a bucket in S3 for storing our music files.
2. Create additional metadata that we will need for the files and store the metadata in our songs domain.
3. Save the actual MP3 file to S3.

Creating an S3 bucket

Each S3 bucket has a name associated with it. Please keep in mind that the name of the bucket needs to be unique not just for your AWS account, but across all accounts in S3. This sometimes makes creating a bucket name challenging!

> You must of course be signed up to use Amazon S3 before trying out the code samples in this chapter. We examined in detail how to signup for Amazon's Web Services in *Chapter 2, Getting Started with SimpleDB*. Please review the chapter if you need help with the sign up process.

Creating an S3 bucket with Java

The **Typica** library does not support S3. In this chapter, we are going to use another Java library named **JetS3t**, which provides complete support for using all of the features provided by S3 from within Java programs.

You can download JetS3t from its project page, `https://jets3t.dev.java.net/`. The latest version at the time of writing this chapter is 0.7.2. Download the distribution, and unzip it to a folder of your choice. Add the `jets3t-0.7.2.jar` to your classpath. We are going to use the **S3Service** class to create a connection to S3 and then use the created object for interacting with S3. We are going to connect to S3 with our credentials, similar to the way we have been connecting when using SimpleDB. Once we connect to S3, we create a new bucket by specifying a unique name for the bucket. We will then print out the contents of the newly-created bucket, which should of course be empty. You can also specify access control for the bucket and the objects contained in it. The default access is `private`, which means that only you can access the bucket and the files in it.

```java
try {
    S3Service s3Service = new RestS3Service(new
        AWSCredentials(awsAccessKey, awsSecretAccessKey));
    S3Bucket songsBucket = s3Service.createBucket("packt_songs");
    System.out.println("Created songs bucket: "
        + songsBucket.getName());
    S3Object[] objects = s3Service.listObjects(songsBucket);
    for (int o = 0; o < objects.length; o++) {
        System.out.println(" " + objects[o].getKey());
    }
} catch (S3ServiceException ex) {
    System.out.println(ex.getMessage());
}
```

Creating an S3 bucket with PHP

SDB-PHP is based on an API called **S3-PHP** by Donovan Schonknecht. S3-PHP can be downloaded from `http://undesigned.org.za/2007/10/22/amazon-s3-php-class`.

Like SDB-PHP, we will use the same key/secret key include (`config.inc.php`).

```
// ACL flags
const ACL_PRIVATE = 'private';
const ACL_PUBLIC_READ = 'public-read';
const ACL_PUBLIC_READ_WRITE = 'public-read-write';
const ACL_AUTHENTICATED_READ = 'authenticated-read';

$s3 = new S3(awsAccessKey, awsSecretKey);

// Create a bucket with public read access
$s3->putBucket($bucketName, S3::ACL_PUBLIC_READ);
```

When uploading a file to S3, the folder and the file each have an access control policy. The two most common are the full public access (the file can be accessed by a URL) and authenticated user where the key and secret key are needed to access the file.

Creating an S3 bucket with Python

Boto provides excellent support for interacting with S3. The interface is very similar to how we have been using boto for SimpleDB in this book. The first thing we are going to do is connect to S3 with our credentials, similar to the way we have been connecting when using SimpleDB. Before you use boto, you must of course set up your environment so that boto can find your AWS Access key identifiers. Set up two environmental variables to point to each of the keys as we have done before.

```
$ export AWS_ACCESS_KEY_ID=Your_AWS_Access_Key_ID
$ export AWS_SECRET_ACCESS_KEY=Your_AWS_Secret_Access_Key
```

Now connect to S3 using boto.

```
>>> import boto
>>>
>>> s3_connection = boto.connect_s3()
>>>
```

Create a new S3 bucket by specifying a name for the bucket. We are not providing a location for the bucket, which means it will be created in the U.S. region by default.

```
>>>
>>> s3_connection.create_bucket('packt_songs')
<Bucket: packt_songs>
>>>
```

Let us now retrieve the newly-created bucket and list the contents of the bucket that will of course be empty as we have not yet stored any files in it.

```
>>>
>>> songs_bkt = s3_connection.get_bucket('packt_songs')
>>>
>>> songs_list = songs_bkt.list()
>>>
>>> for song in songs_list:
...        print song.name
...
>>>
```

Creating additional metadata

In order to store the associated song file for a song, we will need a few additional attributes:

- **File key**: A unique name for the file stored in S3. This is the key to the file in S3.
- **File name**: We need to store the actual filename of the MP3 file for the song.

We can make it expansive and add lots of other attributes such as file extensions, custom header data, and so on, but we are going to keep this simple so the concepts are clear and add these two attributes. The file key needs to be unique as it is also the key to the actual stored file in S3. The simple way would be to use the song name, but that will not work if you have more than one song with same title. We will use a MD5 hash that is generated from the name of the song, name of the artist, and year. This should be unique enough for our purpose, and will be stored as part of the metadata for the song in SimpleDB.

Creating additional metadata with Java

We will use the support already available within Java using the `java.security.*` package to create an MD5 digest. Here is one way to create the digest in Java:

```
try {
    MessageDigest md5 = MessageDigest.getInstance("MD5");
    md5.update("SimpleDB is awesome!".getBytes());
    BigInteger hash = new BigInteger(1, md5.digest());
    System.out.println(hash.toString(16));
} catch (NoSuchAlgorithmException e) {
    e.printStackTrace();
}
```

We will add the additional attributes to our existing songs in the `songs` domain. We will accomplish that by writing some Java code to go through each item in our domain, generating the hash for the key for the file located in this directory, and updating the attributes. We will do the actual uploading of the song file to S3 in the next section.

```
//SimpleDB sdb = new SimpleDB(awsAccessId, awsSecretKey, true);
try {
    Domain domain = sdb.getDomain("songs");
    MessageDigest md5 = MessageDigest.getInstance("MD5");

    Item item = domain.getItem("112222222");
    List<ItemAttribute> list = new ArrayList<ItemAttribute>();
    md5.update("My Way Frank Sinatra".getBytes());
    BigInteger hash = new BigInteger(1, md5.digest());
    list.add(new ItemAttribute("FileKey", hash.toString(16), false));
    list.add(new ItemAttribute("FileName", "My Way.mp3", false));
    item.putAttributes(list);

    item = domain.getItem("089997979");
    list = new ArrayList<ItemAttribute>();
    md5.update("Hotel California Gipsy Kings".getBytes());
    hash = new BigInteger(1, md5.digest());
    list.add(new ItemAttribute("FileKey", hash.toString(16), false));
    list.add(new ItemAttribute("FileName", "Hotel California.mp3",
        false));
    item.putAttributes(list);

    item = domain.getItem("982411114");
    list = new ArrayList<ItemAttribute>();
    md5.update("Geraldine Glasvegas".getBytes());
    hash = new BigInteger(1, md5.digest());
    list.add(new ItemAttribute("FileKey", hash.toString(16), false));
```

```
list.add(new ItemAttribute("FileName", "Geraldine.mp3", false));
item.putAttributes(list);

item = domain.getItem("6767969119");
list = new ArrayList<ItemAttribute>();
md5.update("Transmission Joy Division".getBytes());
hash = new BigInteger(1, md5.digest());
list.add(new ItemAttribute("FileKey", hash.toString(16), false));
list.add(new ItemAttribute("FileName", "Transmission.mp3",
    false));
item.putAttributes(list);

item = domain.getItem("6721309888");
list = new ArrayList<ItemAttribute>();
md5.update("Guzarish Ghazini".getBytes());
hash = new BigInteger(1, md5.digest());
list.add(new ItemAttribute("FileKey", hash.toString(16), false));
list.add(new ItemAttribute("FileName", "Guzarish.mp3", false));
item.putAttributes(list);

item = domain.getItem("0923424244");
list = new ArrayList<ItemAttribute>();
md5.update("So What Miles Davis".getBytes());
hash = new BigInteger(1, md5.digest());
list.add(new ItemAttribute("FileKey", hash.toString(16), false));
list.add(new ItemAttribute("FileName", "So What.mp3", false));
item.putAttributes(list);

item = domain.getItem("5697878778");
list = new ArrayList<ItemAttribute>();
md5.update("Allison Pixies".getBytes());
hash = new BigInteger(1, md5.digest());
list.add(new ItemAttribute("FileKey", hash.toString(16), false));
list.add(new ItemAttribute("FileName", "Allison.mp3", false));
item.putAttributes(list);

item = domain.getItem("7233929292");
list = new ArrayList<ItemAttribute>();
md5.update("Pride Syntax".getBytes());
hash = new BigInteger(1, md5.digest());
list.add(new ItemAttribute("FileKey", hash.toString(16), false));
list.add(new ItemAttribute("FileName", "Pride.mp3", false));
item.putAttributes(list);

item = domain.getItem("5656600009");
list = new ArrayList<ItemAttribute>();
md5.update("Acapulco Neil Diamond".getBytes());
hash = new BigInteger(1, md5.digest());
```

```
    list.add(new ItemAttribute("FileKey", hash.toString(16), false));
    list.add(new ItemAttribute("FileName", "Acapulco.mp3", false));
    item.putAttributes(list);

    item = domain.getItem("1002380899");
    list = new ArrayList<ItemAttribute>();
    md5.update("Scream in Blue Midnight Oil".getBytes());
    hash = new BigInteger(1, md5.digest());
    list.add(new ItemAttribute("FileKey", hash.toString(16), false));
    list.add(new ItemAttribute("FileName", "Scream in Blue.mp3",
        false));
    item.putAttributes(list);
} catch (NoSuchAlgorithmException ex) {
    System.out.println(ex.getMessage());
} catch (SDBException ex) {
    System.out.println(ex.getMessage());
}
```

Creating additional metadata with PHP

We will do the fields in PHP in a slightly different way. `FileName` will have the filename while `FileKey` will have the URL of the file. This approach is useful if you want to store songs in different buckets. The bucket we created before is publicly accessible and when we put in the song, we will also set the access to public read. The `FileName` for storing in S3 is the item name dot song title. This approach would only prevent two identical songs uploaded to the same bucket and same item name.

We will discuss the code in detail in the *Uploading the songs to S3* section with PHP, as the approach is different than the Java and Python examples.

Creating additional metadata with Python

Python includes the `hashlib` module that makes it easy to create MD5 hash digests. It also supports algorithms other than MD5 for the hashing, such as **sha1**, **sha224**, **sha256**, **sha384**, and **sha512**. Here is an example of how to create a MD5 digest:

```
>>>
>>> import hashlib
>>>
>>> m = hashlib.md5()
>>>
>>> m.update("SimpleDB is awesome!")
>>>
```

```
>>> m.hexdigest()

'208bb1e58580e0a74d856ccbef3a3269'

>>>
```

The song MP3 files themselves are stored on the filesystem. In my case, they are all named with the convention—`the name of the song.mp3`. So that means a file listing of the songs on my laptop looks like this:

```
000                                    Default                              

Prabhakar-2:songs prabhakar$ ls -al
total 220280
drwxr-xr-x  12 prabhakar   prabhakar       408 Nov 21 15:44 .
drwxr-xr-x  38 prabhakar   prabhakar      1292 Nov 21 15:41 ..
-rw-r--r--   1 prabhakar   prabhakar   5448961 Nov 17  2008 Acapulco.mp3
-rw-r--r--@  1 prabhakar   prabhakar   2714704 May 26 02:12 Allison.mp3
-rw-r--r--   1 prabhakar   prabhakar   5501257 Sep  3 13:09 Geraldine.mp3
-rw-r--r--   1 prabhakar   prabhakar  10136690 Jan 11  2009 Guzarish.mp3
-rw-r--r--   1 prabhakar   prabhakar  11102885 Dec 23  2007 Hotel California.mp3
-rw-r--r--   1 prabhakar   prabhakar   6882940 Nov 10 11:15 My Way.mp3
-rw-r--r--   1 prabhakar   prabhakar   5460059 Oct 31 11:00 Pride.mp3
-rw-r--r--   1 prabhakar   prabhakar   7997339 Aug 19 09:45 Scream in Blue.mp3
-rw-r--r--   1 prabhakar   prabhakar  50463687 Sep 20  2008 So What.mp3
-rw-r--r--   1 prabhakar   prabhakar   7049460 Dec  3  2007 Transmission.mp3
Prabhakar-2:songs prabhakar$ 
```

Now we need to add the additional attributes to our existing songs in the `songs` domain. We will accomplish that by writing some Python code to go through each item in our domain, generating the hash for the key for the file located in the directory we created, and updating the attributes. We will do the actual uploading of the song file to S3 in the next section.

```
>>>
>>> for item in songs.select("SELECT * FROM `songs`"):
...     item.update({'FileKey' : hashlib.md5("%s %s" %(item['Song'],
item['Artist'])).hexdigest(), 'FileName' : "%s.mp3" %(item['Song'])})
...     item.save()
...
>>>
```

Let us list out the `songs` domain to ensure that we updated the attributes correctly.

```
>>>
>>> for item in songs.select("SELECT * FROM `songs`"):
...     print item.name, item
...
```

```
112222222 {u'Rating': [u'****', u'Excellent', u'4 stars'], u'Artist':
u'Frank Sinatra', u'FileKey': u'b194a34e3340bc1e7df4e8b92a6b95d3',
u'Song': u'My Way', u'FileName': u'My Way.mp3', u'Year': u'2002',
u'Genre': u'Easy Listening'}

089997979 {u'Rating': u'****', u'Song': u'Hotel California', u'FileKey':
u'7c41966c82688ed375fdd0f36cd85444', u'Artist': u'Gipsy Kings',
u'FileName': u'Hotel California.mp3', u'Genre': u'World'}

982411114 {u'Rating': u'*****', u'Artist': u'Glasvegas', u'FileKey': u'
e7b6ac5cc4c38946afff7aceefa4931b', u'Song': u'Geraldine', u'FileName':
u'Geraldine.mp3', u'Year': u'2008', u'Genre': [u'Rock', u'Alternative']}

6767969119 {u'Rating': [u'Excellent', u'*****'], u'Artist': u'Joy
Division', u'FileKey': u'5e0c3a6fae1dda6aaf6ae32506d41208', u'Song':
u'Transmission', u'FileName': u'Transmission.mp3', u'Year': u'1981',
u'Genre': u'Alternative'}

6721309888 {u'Rating': [u'Not rated', u'Awful'], u'Artist': u'Ghazini',
u'FileKey': u'ba27acdb613e5f0617d81b4d274a042c', u'Song': u'Guzarish',
u'FileName': u'Guzarish.mp3', u'Year': u'2008', u'Genre': u'Bollywood'}

0923424244 {u'Rating': [u'*****', u'Wow!'], u'Artist': u'Miles Davis',
u'FileKey': u'ee8f800f28b4962803d0be82cf29a2b3', u'Song': u'So What',
u'FileName': u'So What.mp3', u'Year': u'1959', u'Genre': u'Jazz'}

5697878778 {u'Rating': [u'4 stars', u'****'], u'Artist': u'Pixies',
u'FileKey': u'98e1168a692a881242b3497488752f75', u'Song': u'Allison',
u'FileName': u'Allison.mp3', u'Year': u'1990', u'Genre': u'Alternative'}

7233929292 {u'Rating': [u'Excellent', u'*****'], u'Song': u'Pride',
u'FileKey': u'75b701f9b040429b4f995646c1b8b1d1', u'Artist': u'Syntax',
u'FileName': u'Pride.mp3', u'Genre': [u'Alternative', u'Electronic']}

5656600009 {u'Rating': [u'1 star', u'*', u'Avoid'], u'Artist': u'Neil
Diamond', u'FileKey':u'a5e2df2c642f5ec071544e1883b87534', u'Song':
u'Acapulco', u'FileName': u'Acapulco.mp3', u'Year': u'1980', u'Genre':
u'Soundtrack'}

1002380899 {u'Rating': [u'***', u'3 stars'], u'Artist': u'Midnight Oil',
u'FileKey': u'd703e82cc0ab7cf1457dc815f5a7be89', u'Song': u'Scream in
Blue', u'FileName': u'Scream in Blue.mp3', u'Year': u'1983', u'Genre':
u'Rock'}

>>>
```

All our songs now have a `FileKey` and a `FileName` attribute, and we have all the information we need. This is one of the truly impressive things about SimpleDB—the ability to dynamically add new attributes to an existing item. No schemas to worry about, no upgrades, just a simple web services call! No database administrators sitting on your shoulder about migrations! Any time that your use case changes, or you need to store additional information, it is extremely easy.

Uploading the songs to S3

We will now upload the MP3 files to S3. The Java and Python examples will use a hashed filename as the key while the PHP code will use a name composed of the item name and the MP3 filename.

Uploading the songs to S3 with Java

We have all the metadata for our songs in place in SimpleDB. Now all we have to do is upload each corresponding file itself to our S3 bucket that we created earlier in this chapter.

```
try {
    S3Service s3Service = new RestS3Service(new
AWSCredentials(awsAccessKey, awsSecretAccessKey));
    S3Bucket songsBucket = s3Service.getBucket("packt_songs");
    File folder = new File("/songs_folder");
    File[] listOfFiles = folder.listFiles();
    for (int i = 0; i < listOfFiles.length; i++) {
        if (listOfFiles[i].isFile()) {
            S3Object fileObject = new S3Object(listOfFiles[i]);
            s3Service.putObject(songsBucket, fileObject);
        }
    }
} catch (NoSuchAlgorithmException ex) {
    System.out.println(ex.getMessage());
} catch (IOException ex) {
    System.out.println(ex.getMessage());
} catch (S3ServiceException ex) {
    System.out.println(ex.getMessage());
}
```

Uploading the songs to S3 with PHP

Uploading the song is broken into two programs: s3upload.php and s3uploader. php. The first is used to select the parameters of the upload: the file, bucket, and item to upload to. The second program using the parameters from the first program does the actual upload.

The steps involved are as follows:

s3upload.php

1. Display list of buckets.
2. Display list of items including a link to the song if it has been uploaded already.
3. User selects an MP3 file to upload.
4. User selects a bucket.
5. User selects an item name.

s3uploader.php

1. File uploaded to temp area.
2. getAttributes of item song title.
3. Compute FileName as item name + song title.
4. Copy temp file to S3, naming it with the FileName from step 3.
5. Add the attribute FileName with the value from step 3. If a previous FileName exists, replace it.
6. Add the attribute FileKey with the URL to the file. If a previous FileKey exists, replace it.

These programs bring together many of the steps covered so far. Let's walk through these one at a time.

After running **Set your key/secret key for the session**, run **Upload MP3 Song to S3**. This is the user interface. This is obviously a very basic user interface but the focus of this sample is on illustrating uploading a file to S3, not good GUI design.

Let the user select a file to upload. The program will call s3uploader.php.

```
<form action="s3uploader.php" method="post"
      enctype="multipart/form-data">
1. Select file: <input type="file" name="file" id="file"><br>
```

List the available buckets. First create an instance of S3 object and echo a list of radio buttons with the bucket name.

```
$s3 = new S3(awsAccessKey, awsSecretKey);
$bucketList = $s3->listBuckets();
foreach ($bucketList as $bucketListName) {
    echo("<input type='radio'
               name='s3bucket'
               value='".$bucketListName."'> "
               .$bucketListName."<br>");
}
```

Now list the available items in the songs domain. If the FileKey has the URL of a previously uploaded MP3 then build a link using the URL in FileKey.

```php
$sdb = new SimpleDB(awsAccessKey, awsSecretKey); // create connection
$domain = "songs";
$sql = "SELECT itemName, Song, FileKey from $domain";
$rest = $sdb->select($domain,$sql);
foreach ($rest as $item) {
    $item_name = $item["Name"];
    $song = $item["Attributes"]["Song"];
    $httpaddr = $item["Attributes"]["FileKey"];
    echo("<input type='radio' name='itemname'
                value='".$item_name."'> ");
    if (empty($httpaddr)) {
        echo($item_name." / ".$song);
    } else {
        echo("<a href='$httpaddr'>");
        echo($item_name." / ".$song);
        echo("</a>");
    }
    echo("<br>");
}
<br><input type="submit" name="submit" value="4. Click to upload">
</form>
```

Now the user selects from: 1. File, 2. Bucket, and 3. Item and then clicks on 4., the submit button.

The file is uploaded to a temporary location. PHP provides several variables with information on the file. $_FILES["file"] has elements for type, size, and name. The sample has a basic filter to permit only certain file types to be uploaded. Next is a check for maximum file size. Again this is not required but is protection against a user uploading gigantic files. The S3-PHP upload does not support an upload of 2 GB or larger on a 32-bit PHP server.

```php
// add types permitted into the string
$allowedtypes = "|image/gif|image/jpeg|image/pjpeg|image/png|
    audio/mpeg|text/plain|application/pdf|";
$fileType = "|".$_FILES["file"]["type"]."|";
if (!stristr($allowedtypes,$fileType)) {
    die("Invalid file type: ".$_FILES["file"]["type"]);
}
// Set maximum file size that you permit to be uploaded
if ($_FILES["file"]["size"] > 2000000) {
```

```
        die("File too large: ".$_FILES["file"]["size"]);
    }
    // upload file to temporary upload area
    if ($_FILES["file"]["error"] > 0) {
        die("Error: " . $_FILES["file"]["error"]);
    } else    {
        echo "Upload: " . $_FILES["file"]["name"] . "<br />";
        echo "Type: " . $_FILES["file"]["type"] . "<br />";
        echo "Size: " . ($_FILES["file"]["size"] / 1024) . " Kb<br />";
        echo "Stored in: " . $_FILES["file"]["tmp_name"]."<p>";
    }
```

The output this code produces is as follows:

```
Upload: MyWay.mp3
Type: audio/mpeg
Size: 17.142578125 Kb
Stored in: /tmp/phpg4AMf0
```

The variables for the item name, address to the temporary file, and the name by which it will be known as in S3 are created.

```
$itemName = $_POST["itemname"];

$uploadFile = $_FILES["file"]["tmp_name"]; // Temporary file name
$uploadName = $itemName.".".$_FILES["file"]["name"]; // S3 file name
```

The program next validates that the S3 bucket exists.

```
// List your buckets: check if passed bucket needs to be created
echo "S3::listBuckets(): <br>\n";
$bucketList = $s3->listBuckets();
$bucketfound = false;
foreach ($bucketList as $bucketListName) {
  if ($bucketListName == $bucketName)   {
    echo("   ".$bucketListName." FOUND<br>\n");
    $bucketfound = true;
  } else {
    echo("   ".$bucketListName."<br>\n");
  }
}
echo("<br>\n");

if (!$bucketfound) { // if bucket not found try creating it
  // Create a bucket with public read access
  if ($s3->putBucket($bucketName, S3::ACL_PUBLIC_READ)) {
    echo "Created bucket {$bucketName}".PHP_EOL."<p>\n";
    $bucketfound = true;
```

```
    } else {
       echo "S3::putBucket(): Unable to create bucket '{$bucketName}' (it
may be owned by someone else)\n";
    }
}
```

Now that the bucket is found, copy the file from the temporary storage to S3.

```
    if ($s3->putObjectFile($uploadFile, $bucketName, $uploadName,
S3::ACL_PUBLIC_READ)) {
       echo "S3::putObjectFile(): File copied to {$bucketName}/".$upload
Name."<p>\n";
```

By using `ACL_PUBLIC_READ` the code is setting public access to read the file. Next, query the information on the file, which is now in S3.

```
// Get object info
$info = $s3->getObjectInfo($bucketName, $uploadName);
// Build URL to the uploaded file
$httpaddr = "http://".$bucketName.".s3.amazonaws.com/".$uploadName;
echo("Link to download: <a href='$httpaddr'>$httpaddr</a><br>");
echo "S3::getObjecInfo(): Info for {$bucketName}/
    ".$uploadName."<br>\n";
foreach ($info as $fattribute => $fvalue) { // split attributes
    echo("   ".$fattribute."=".$fvalue."<br>");
}
```

The last step is to add the `FileName` and `FileKey` attributes to the `songs` domain.

```
$sdb = new SimpleDB(awsAccessKey, awsSecretKey); // create connection
echo "<br>Update SimpleDB item $itemName<br>";
$putAttributesRequest["FileName"] = array("value" => $uploadName,
"replace" => "true"); // File name
$putAttributesRequest["FileKey"] = array("value" => $httpaddr,
"replace" => "true"); // Address of the file

$domain = "songs";
$rest = $sdb->putAttributes($domain,$itemName,$putAttributesRequest);
if ($rest) {
  echo("Record $itemName updated");
  echo("RequestId: ".$sdb->RequestId."<br>");
  echo("BoxUsage: ".$sdb->BoxUsage." = " .
SimpleDB::displayUsage($sdb->BoxUsage)."<br>");
} else {
  echo("Record $itemName FAILED<br>");
  echo("ErrorCode: ".$sdb->ErrorCode."<p>");
}
```

Uploading the songs to S3 with Python

Uploading is very straightforward when using boto. We will loop through each item, look for a file named using our convention, and upload it to S3 using the generated hash as the key. The songs will be uploaded to the `packt_songs` bucket that we created earlier. Sounds much harder than it actually is, especially when using Python!

```
>>>
>>> songs_bkt = s3_connection.get_bucket('packt_songs')
>>>
>>> for item in songs.select("SELECT * FROM `songs`"):
...     key = songs_bkt.new_key(item['FileKey'])
...     f = open ("/Users/prabhakar/Documents/SimpleDB Book/songs/%s.mp3"
%(item['Song']))
...     key.set_contents_from_file(f)
...     f.close()
...
>>>
```

Let us list our bucket and make sure that we did get them all in.

```
>>>
>>> songs_list = songs_bkt.list()
>>> for song in songs_list:
...     print song.name
...
5e0c3a6fae1dda6aaf6ae32506d41208
75b701f9b040429b4f995646c1b8b1d1
7c41966c82688ed375fdd0f36cd85444
98e1168a692a881242b3497488752f75
a5e2df2c642f5ec071544e1883b87534
b194a34e3340bc1e7df4e8b92a6b95d3
ba27acdb613e5f0617d81b4d274a042c
d703e82cc0ab7cf1457dc815f5a7be89
e7b6ac5cc4c38946afff7aceefa4931b
ee8f800f28b4962803d0be82cf29a2b3
>>>
```

The above list shows the names of all the keys that we have uploaded. That's it. Now we are all done. Our songs domain has all the metadata and the songs themselves are in S3!

Retrieving the files from S3

Downloading our files is quite simple. We can use any of the libraries for downloading the files. S3 supports two ways to access files: a file can be set with a permission of public (that is everyone can view it) or private (the key and secret key are required for access).

In the Java and Python examples, the API uses the default private access; in the PHP sample full public access is used. The S3-PHP API support private access also.

Retrieving the files from S3 with Java

We will use Jets3t for retrieving the files from S3. Here is a quick way to download the files using Java.

```
try {
S3Service s3Service = new RestS3Service(new
AWSCredentials(awsAccessKey, awsSecretAccessKey));
    S3ServiceSimpleMulti simpleMulti = new S3ServiceSimpleMulti(s3Ser
vice);
    S3Bucket songsBucket = s3Service.getBucket("packt_songs");
    S3Object[] objects = new S3Object[10];
    simpleMulti.getObjects(songsBucket, objects);
    DownloadPackage[] downloadPackages = new DownloadPackage[10];
    downloadPackages[0] = new DownloadPackage(objects[0],
            new File(objects[0].getKey()));
    downloadPackages[1] = new DownloadPackage(objects[1],
            new File(objects[1].getKey()));
    downloadPackages[2] = new DownloadPackage(objects[2],
            new File(objects[2].getKey()));
    downloadPackages[3] = new DownloadPackage(objects[3],
            new File(objects[3].getKey()));
    downloadPackages[4] = new DownloadPackage(objects[4],
            new File(objects[4].getKey()));
    downloadPackages[5] = new DownloadPackage(objects[5],
            new File(objects[5].getKey()));
    downloadPackages[6] = new DownloadPackage(objects[6],
            new File(objects[6].getKey()));
    downloadPackages[7] = new DownloadPackage(objects[7],
            new File(objects[7].getKey()));
```

```
downloadPackages[8] = new DownloadPackage(objects[8],
        new File(objects[8].getKey()));
downloadPackages[9] = new DownloadPackage(objects[9],
        new File(objects[9].getKey()));
simpleMulti.downloadObjects(songsBucket, downloadPackages);
} catch (S3ServiceException ex) {
    System.out.println(ex.getMessage());
}
```

Retrieving the files from S3 with PHP

Using the same listing technique as `s3upload.php` we can list the items and links to the songs.

```
$sdb = new SimpleDB(awsAccessKey, awsSecretKey); // create connection
$domain = "songs";
$sql = "SELECT itemName, Song, FileKey from $domain";
$rest = $sdb->select($domain,$sql);

foreach ($rest as $item) {
  $item_name = $item["Name"];
  $song = $item["Attributes"]["Song"];
  $httpaddr = $item["Attributes"]["FileKey"];

  if (empty($httpaddr)) {
    echo($item_name." / ".$song);
  } else {
    echo("<a href='$httpaddr'>");
    echo($item_name." / ".$song);
    echo("</a>");
  }
  echo("<br>");
}
```

Now it is time to play the song. Select S3 MP3 Song Player from the menu. The song items that have `FileKey` are listed.

```
$sdb = new SimpleDB(awsAccessKey, awsSecretKey);
  // create connection
$domain = "songs";
$sql = "SELECT itemName, Song, FileKey from $domain WHERE FileKey IS
NOT NULL";
$rest = $sdb->select($domain,$sql);
foreach ($rest as $item) {
    $item_name = $item["Name"];
    $song = $item["Attributes"]["Song"];
```

```
        $httpaddr = $item["Attributes"]["FileKey"];
        echo("<input type='radio' name='songaddr'
                    value='".$httpaddr."'> ");
      echo($item_name." / ".$song);
      echo("<br>");
    }
```

When a song is selected the URL is posted. Using Martin Laine's Flash Audio Player (`http://wpaudioplayer.com/standalone`), the program feeds the URL and a flash player is created. Then just click on the player to hear the song.

This code is placed in the header:

```
<head>
<script type="text/javascript" src="audio-player/audio-player.js"></
script>
<script type="text/javascript">
    AudioPlayer.setup("audio-player/player.swf", {
        width: 290
    });
</script>
</head>
```

The following code creates the flash MP3 player if a song URL is passed.

```
if (!empty($_POST["songaddr"])) { // fetch bucket name
?>
    <p id="audioplayer_1">Alternative content</p>
    <script type="text/javascript">
        AudioPlayer.embed("audioplayer_1",
            {soundFile: "<?php echo($_POST["songaddr"]) ?>"});
    </script>
<?php } ?>
```

So we have a complete system to upload a song, add to the SimpleDB item, a player based on S3, and SimpleDB items.

Retrieving the files from S3 with Python

We can use boto itself to download it or even generate a time-sensitive URL for downloading it. We are going to look at both of these ways for download.

First let us download the file using boto. We will download the file to the specified directory.

```
>>>
>>> for item in songs.select("SELECT * FROM `songs` WHERE Song='So
What'"):
...        key = songs_bkt.get_key(item['FileKey'])
...        f = open ("/Users/prabhakar/Documents/SimpleDB Book/%s.mp3"
%(item['Song']), 'w')
...        key.get_contents_to_file(f)
...        f.close()
...
```

We can also use boto to generate a URL for the file and specify a time period of validity for the URL. At the end of this specified time, the URL will no longer work. Here we will use boto to create the URL.

 Please keep in mind that anyone can use this URL to download the file. It will expire after the time period specified, but within the time period anyone can use this URL to download the file.

```
>>> for item in songs.select("SELECT * FROM `songs` WHERE
Song='Allison'"):
...        key = songs_bkt.get_key(item['FileKey'])
...        print key.generate_url(3600)
...
https://packt_songs.s3.amazonaws.
:443/98e1168a692a881242b3497488752f75?Signature=cCkb71GKEcEO0ha80aPYx4A%2
B3ok%3D&Expires=1258855566&AWSAccessKeyId=BCIAJCQ568ASHKIK
>>>
```

This URL uses the HTTP addressable form of our `packt_songs` bucket `https://packt_songs.s3.amazonaws.com`, for retrieving the file. The actual object that we are retrieving is the MP3 file with the key `98e1168a692a881242b3497488752f75`. You can use any web client to retrieve this file!

Summary

In this chapter, we discussed Amazon S3 and its use for storing large files. We modified our songs domain to add additional metadata including a file key that was later used for naming the MP3 file uploaded to S3. The example used in this chapter shows you a simple way to store metadata on SimpleDB while storing associated content that is in the form of binary files on Amazon S3. In the next chapter, we are going to look at queries and how to tune them using the box usage value that is returned by the response to every SimpleDB request.

8
Tuning and Usage Costs

SimpleDB queries can be tuned in order to provide the best performance as well as cost effectiveness. In order to perform any kind of tuning, we need to first examine the concept of **BoxUsage** provided as a part of the response to every SimpleDB request. In this chapter, we will discuss the BoxUsage and look at how it varies for different kinds of SimpleDB operations. We will also look at usage costs and usage activity reports that are provided by AWS. We will also talk about the concept of partitioning.

BoxUsage

Each request made to SimpleDB returns a **BoxUsage** value as part of the response. This response indicates the amount of system resources that were utilized by that specific operation. This value can be used to figure out the cost of making any kind of a request to SimpleDB, and can thus be used to tune queries.

 The higher the BoxUsage value, the more expensive the request made to SimpleDB.

The value of BoxUsage is always consistent for operations such as creating a domain, but in the case of Select requests that are usually used for querying SimpleDB, the BoxUsage values are normalized and are supposed to reflect two parameters that categorize your SimpleDB data:

- Your dataset and the data that is contained within it
- The complexity of the query that you are making to SimpleDB for retrieving your data

This enables one to optimize and tune their queries using the BoxUsage value. This value is not affected by what other users are doing when utilized in the context of making Select queries, and lets you choose queries that can provide you with the best possible performance.

BoxUsage does not include the costs for bandwidth or storage.

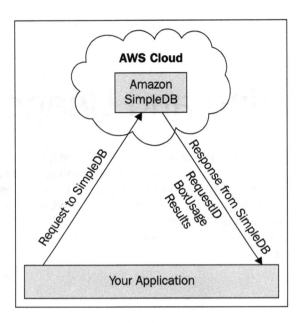

Computing costs using BoxUsage

BoxUsage is reported by SimpleDB as the portion of a machine hour that is used to complete a specific request. The actual measurement is normalized to the hourly capacity of a 2007 1.7 GHz Xeon processor. The charges are based on the amount of the machine capacity used to complete the particular request (SELECT, GET, PUT, and so on). The costs are of course different based on the region that your SimpleDB data resides in—U.S. or EU.

The current pricing for machine utilization in the U.S. region is:

- The first 25 Amazon SimpleDB machine hours consumed per month are free
- $0.140 per Amazon SimpleDB machine hour consumed thereafter

The current pricing for machine utilization in the EU region is:

- The first 25 Amazon SimpleDB machine hours consumed per month are free
- $0.154 per Amazon SimpleDB machine hour consumed thereafter

Let us compute the hypothetical cost for a BoxUsage of 30 hours over the course of a single month. These 30 hours are the accumulated sum of the BoxUsage values for all of your requests made for this month.

U.S. region
The first 25 machine hours are free.
(30 - 25) hours x $0.14 per machine-hour x 1 month = $0.70 for the month
EU region
The first 25 machine hours are free.
(30 -25) hours x $0.154 per machine-hour x 1 month = $0.77 for the month

Usage reports

You can view the monthly usage activity for each of your Amazon web services, including SimpleDB on your account page.

Account Activity

View Previous Statement

Summary of This Month's Activity as of November 28, 2009
Billing Cycle for this Report: November 1 - November 30, 2009
AWS service usage charges on this page currently show activity through approximately 11/28/2009 16:59 GMT.

Expand All | Collapse All

Rate	Usage	Totals
Amazon CloudFront View/Edit Service		
	View Usage Report	0.00
Amazon Elastic Compute Cloud View/Edit Service		
	View Usage Report	0.00
Amazon Elastic MapReduce View/Edit Service		
	View Usage Report	0.00
Amazon Relational Database Service View/Edit Service		
	View Usage Report	0.00
Amazon Simple Queue Service View/Edit Service		
	View Usage Report	0.01
Amazon Simple Storage Service View/Edit Service		
	View Usage Report	2.54
Amazon SimpleDB View/Edit Service		
	View Usage Report	0.00
Taxes Estimated Taxes (Due December 1, 2009)		0.00

You can expand the **Amazon SimpleDB** tab to view its costs.

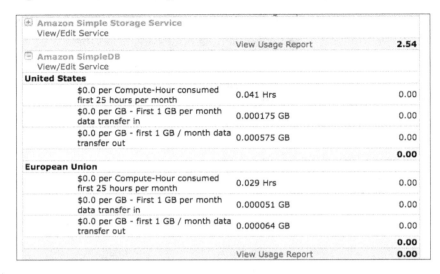

This gives you the overall cost for that month for using SimpleDB. You can drill down to the particulars of your SimpleDB usage by clicking on the **View Usage Report** on that page. That will take you to a page where you can select the time period of choice and download a detailed usage report in either XML or CSV format.

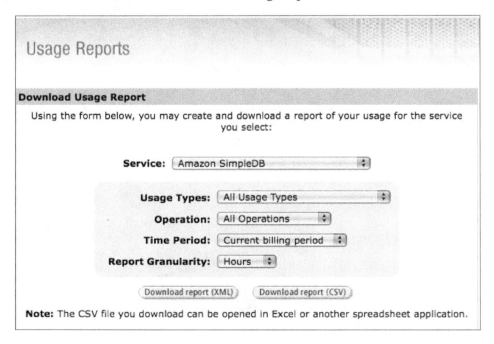

If you choose to download the report, it will contain a list of all the operations for SimpleDB performed by your account. Here is a sample operation that may be listed in your report:

```
<OperationUsage>
    <ServiceName>AmazonSimpleDB</ServiceName>
    <OperationName>ListDomains</OperationName>
    <UsageType>BoxUsage</UsageType>
    <StartTime>11/01/09 04:00:00</StartTime>
    <EndTime>11/01/09 05:00:00</EndTime>
    <UsageValue>1.43518e-05</UsageValue>
</OperationUsage>
<OperationUsage>
    <ServiceName>AmazonSimpleDB</ServiceName>
    <OperationName>ListDomains</OperationName>
    <UsageType>Requests</UsageType>
    <StartTime>11/01/09 04:00:00</StartTime>
    <EndTime>11/01/09 05:00:00</EndTime>
    <UsageValue>2</UsageValue>
</OperationUsage>
```

This shows that between 4:00 A.M. and 5:00 A.M. on November 1, 2009, you made two requests for listing your SimpleDB domains, and the BoxUsage for it was 0.0000143518. You can go through the entire report and see each and every operation that you used for that time period. For instance, for the preceding list domains operations, there is also an associated EC2 bandwidth cost.

```
<OperationUsage>
    <ServiceName>AmazonSimpleDB</ServiceName>
    <OperationName>ListDomains</OperationName>
    <UsageType>EC2DataTransfer-Out-Bytes</UsageType>
    <StartTime>11/01/09 04:00:00</StartTime>
    <EndTime>11/01/09 05:00:00</EndTime>
    <UsageValue>830</UsageValue>
</OperationUsage>
<OperationUsage>
    <ServiceName>AmazonSimpleDB</ServiceName>
    <OperationName>ListDomains</OperationName>
    <UsageType>EC2DataTransfer-In-Bytes</UsageType>
    <StartTime>11/01/09 04:00:00</StartTime>
    <EndTime>11/01/09 05:00:00</EndTime>
    <UsageValue>651</UsageValue>
</OperationUsage>
```

Similarly, you also have the data transfer costs. Currently SimpleDB has a free tier, which is really enticing and helpful if you are looking into using SimpleDB or exploring it.

 There are no charges on the first 25 machine hours, 1 GB of data transfer, and 1 GB of storage that you consume every month on SimpleDB. Per AWS calculations, approximately 2,000,000 GET or SELECT API requests can be completed per month within the free tier. Until June 30, 2010 all data transfers into Amazon SimpleDB are free of charge.

BoxUsage — Java

Typica provides a simple way to access the **BoxUsage** value along with the `RequestId`, when you query SimpleDB. In the following sample, we will list all our domains and print the associated **BoxUsage** value as well as the `RequestId` for the operation.

```
public static void main(String[] args) {
    SimpleDB sdb = new SimpleDB(awsAccessId, awsSecretKey, true);
    try {
        ListDomainsResult domainsResult = sdb.listDomains();
        System.out.println("RequestID : "
            + domainsResult.getRequestId());
        System.out.println("Box Usage : "
            + domainsResult.getBoxUsage());
    } catch (SDBException ex) {
        System.out.println(ex.getMessage());
    }
}
```

This sample will print the following values to the console:

RequestID : a5d9fd56-f91a-8130-a7b9-0e05a2e66fb9

Box Usage : 0.0000071759

The usage value is a little difficult to comprehend and compare with other values. So we need a simple way to convert this into more human-readable format. We are going to call this the **micro-hours** or **muH** and compute this number by multiplying a usage value by 1000000. Here is a simple Java method that does this conversion.

```
private static String getBoxUsageAsMicroHours(String origBoxUsage) {
    return "" + (Double.parseDouble(origBoxUsage) * 1000000);
}
```

Let us modify our previous sample to use the converted value for usage.

```
public static void main(String[] args) {
    SimpleDB sdb = new SimpleDB(awsAccessId, awsSecretKey, true);
    try {
        ListDomainsResult domainsResult = sdb.listDomains();
        System.out.println("RequestID : "
            + domainsResult.getRequestId());
        System.out.println("Box Usage : "
            + domainsResult.getBoxUsage());
        System.out.println("Box Usage (muH): "
            + getBoxUsageAsMicroHours(domainsResult.getBoxUsage()));
    } catch (SDBException ex) {
        System.out.println(ex.getMessage());
    }
}
private static String getBoxUsageAsMicroHours(String origBoxUsage) {
    return "" + (Double.parseDouble(origBoxUsage) * 1000000);
}
```

For comparison, here is the console output when you run this code sample:

```
RequestID : cde017df-324d-913a-e3b5-8ff1eca50ae0

Box Usage : 0.0000071759

Box Usage (muH): 7.1759
```

In the rest of this section, we will take a look at several examples of BoxUsage and how you can utilize it to make your applications faster and cheaper to execute. A caveat with typical is that the library returns BoxUsage values only with query results. This makes it difficult to get the BoxUsage values when you are doing basic operations on the domain or an item. However, in the rest of this chapter both the PHP and Python sections have a nice discussion of the usage values for common domain and item operations. Please refer to those sections for details on these operations.

Cost of Select

All Select queries are not created equally. The costs associated with Select vary depending on the query. Here are some usage values when using different operators/expressions within the Select.

```
public static void main(String[] args) {
    SimpleDB sdb = new SimpleDB(awsAccessId, awsSecretKey, true);
    try {
        Domain domain = sdb.getDomain("songs");
```

```
            String queryString = "SELECT * FROM `songs`
                WHERE Year='1985'";
            QueryWithAttributesResult queryResults = domain
                .selectItems(queryString, null);
            System.out.println("Box Usage (muH): "
                + getBoxUsageAsMicroHours(queryResults.getBoxUsage()));

            queryString = "SELECT * FROM `songs` WHERE Year
                        LIKE '1985%'";
            queryResults = domain.selectItems(queryString, null);
            System.out.println("Box Usage (muH): "
                + getBoxUsageAsMicroHours(queryResults.getBoxUsage()));

            queryString = "SELECT * FROM `songs` WHERE Year
                        LIKE '%1985%'";
            queryResults = domain.selectItems(queryString, null);
            System.out.println("Box Usage (muH): "
                + getBoxUsageAsMicroHours(queryResults.getBoxUsage()));

        } catch (SDBException ex) {
            System.out.println(ex.getMessage());
        }
    }
    private static String getBoxUsageAsMicroHours(String origBoxUsage) {
        return "" + (Double.parseDouble(origBoxUsage) * 1000000);
    }
```

Following are the usage values returned when we run this sample.

Box Usage (muH): 13.72

Box Usage (muH): 13.72

Box Usage (muH): 13.7514

Using the LIKE operation for a string anywhere within the value costs more, as a complete table scan is required to check every record for the substring. The songs domain is small, so this may not be a significant cost difference, but if this were a large domain the costs will add up quickly.

BoxUsage — PHP

All of the programs in the PHP samples return BoxUsage along with the RequestId and the NextToken if required.

Rich Helms: While writing the samples, I found some of the BoxUsage numbers interesting.

```
$sdb = new SimpleDB(awsAccessKey, awsSecretKey);
$item_name = "112222222";
$rest = $sdb->getAttributes($domain,$item_name);
if ($rest) {
    echo "getAttributes for $item_name<pre>";
    print_r($rest);
    echo "</pre><P>";
    echo("RequestId: ".$sdb->RequestId."<br>");
    echo("Total BoxUsage $boxusage = "
         . SimpleDB::displayUsage($boxusage) . "<br>");
    echo("NextToken: ".$sdb->NextToken."<br>");
} else {
    echo("Listing FAILED<br>");
    echo("ErrorCode: ".$sdb->ErrorCode."<p>");
}
```

The sample shows how to access the three values on a successful call and the error code on an unsuccessful call.

Let's look at several examples of BoxUsage and understand how SimpleDB changes for usage can make your application not only faster but cheaper to execute.

Cost of NextToken

In the PHP sample "Backup a Domain", the BoxUsage is totaled up for the run. In backup, an SQL statement is used to define what part of the domain is backed up to S3. A limit can also be added to the SQL to limit how many items are returned in each call to SimpleDB. For the songs domain here are the two extremes.

First select all 11 items in one call.

```
select * from songs
Total BoxUsage 0.0001142976 = 114.3 muH
     114.3 muH
```

In the second example, limit the return to 1 item at a time using `NextToken` to perform the select 11 times.

```
select * from songs limit 1
Total BoxUsage 0.0002514776 = 251.5 muH
     22.9  muH
     22.9  muH
     22.9  muH
     22.9  muH
     22.9  muH
     22.9  muH
     22.9  muH
     22.9  muH
     22.9  muH
     22.9  muH
     22.9  muH
```

Included in SDB-PHP is a function `displayUsage($boxusage)`, which displays the BoxUsage as the number of micro-hours (muH) rounded to one decimal place. This makes comparing two usages easier.

While the second scenario required 11 calls to SimpleDB, it consumed only just over twice the time. The lesson here seems to be that using `NextToken` is not very expensive.

One of the most glaring examples of how different strategies can affect cost is using Select versus `getAttributes` for retrieving the attributes of one item. In the `songs` domain there are two ways to retrieve all of the attributes for item `112222222`: `getAttributes` and Select. As Select is more flexible, the tendency is to use that, but what is the cost? Both `getAttributes` and Select can retrieve an item by its item name.

For example, query all attributes for `112222222` item.

```
$sdb = new SimpleDB(awsAccessKey, awsSecretKey); // create connection
$domain = "songs";
$sdb = new SimpleDB(awsAccessKey, awsSecretKey);
$item_name = "112222222";
$rest = $sdb->getAttributes($domain,$item_name);
echo("BoxUsage: ".$sdb->BoxUsage."<br>");
BoxUsage: 0.0000094182 = 9.4 muH
$rest = $sdb->select($domain,"select * from $domain WHERE itemName() =
'112222222'");
echo("BoxUsage: ".$sdb->BoxUsage."<br>");
BoxUsage: 0.0000228616 = 22.9 muH
2.42738527532 times the cost of using getAttribute
```

So the moral of that program is that Select is 2.4 times as expensive as `getAttribute` when fetching the attributes of ONE item by the item name.

Cost of Select

Certain capabilities of Select have the potential to be expensive. Let's look at several queries using the 11 items in songs.

```
select * from songs where Year='1985'
BoxUsage: 0.0000228616 = 228,616 nh/10

select * from songs where Year LIKE '1985%'
BoxUsage: 0.0000228616 = 228,616 nh/10

select * from songs where Year LIKE '%1985%'
BoxUsage: 0.0000229165 = 229,165 nh/10
```

All of these queries return one record. Equal and begins with LIKE are charged the same, but LIKE for a string anywhere in the value costs more as a complete table scan is required to check every record for the substring. This is on a very small domain so the cost difference is not significant although on a large domain it may not be.

Cost of creating a domain

Creating or deleting a domain is expensive. It consumes BoxUsage of 5,559 muH. If you create a domain and it already exists, you are still charged the cost of creating the domain. A common coding practice is to verify a table exists before writing to it. In SimpleDB if you create a domain that already exists there is no error and the domain remains unchanged. But it is far cheaper in SimpleDB to check if the domain exists rather than creating by default.

```
Domain songs created

BoxUsage: 0.0055590278 = 5,559.0 muH
```

As you can see from this output, creating the `songs` domain is expensive, even if it exists. It is best to check if the domain exists and only create it if it does not exist.

```
Check for the domain's existence with domainMetadata

Domain songs Metadata requested (the domain exists)

BoxUsage: 0.0000071759 = 7.2 muH

Domain songs Metadata requested (does not exist)

BoxUsage: = 0.0 muH

Domain songs created
```

```
BoxUsage: 0.0055590278 = 5,559.0 muH
```

```
11 Records created
```
```
BoxUsage: 0.0001701125 = 170.1 muH
```

Colin Percival in his article *Dissecting SimpleDB BoxUsage*, at http://www. daemonology.net/blog/2008-06-25-dissecting-simpledb-boxusage.html, goes into an interesting analysis of the BoxUsage of the commands available in 2008. The article does not cover Select or batchPutAttributes as they were announced later.

Cost of creating items

Multiple items can be created with putAttributes as well as batchPutAttributes. The first makes a rest call for each item, the second can create 25 items in one call. If you are creating more than one item, my experience is that the batchPutAttributes is cheaper.

```
car1 created
```
```
BoxUsage: 0.0000219961 = 22.0 muH (3 attributes)
```
```
car2 created
```
```
BoxUsage: 0.0000219923 = 22.0 muH (2 attributes)
```
```
car3 created
```
```
BoxUsage: 0.0000220035 = 22.0 muH (4 attributes)
```

```
Total BoxUsage: 0.0000659919 = 66.0 muH
```

Creating all three items in one batchPutAttributes is not only faster but cheaper.

```
Car1, car2, car3 created
```
```
BoxUsage: 0.0000461943 = 46.2 muH
```

BoxUsage — Python

Create a new domain and check the BoxUsage value for it. Unlike the previous sections in PHP and Java, we are going to just use the BoxUsage value as returned from SimpleDB in this section.

```
>>> import boto
>>> sdb_connection = boto.connect_sdb()
>>>
>>> new_domain = sdb_connection.create_domain('tuning')
>>>
>>> print dir(new_domain)
```

```
['BoxUsage', 'CreateDomainResponse', 'RequestId', 'ResponseMetadata',
'__doc__', '__init__', '__iter__', '__module__', '__repr__', '_metadata',
'batch_put_attributes', 'connection', 'delete_attributes', 'delete_item',
'endElement', 'from_xml', 'get_attributes', 'get_item', 'get_metadata',
'name', 'new_item', 'put_attributes', 'query', 'select', 'startElement',
'to_xml']
>>>
>>> new_domain.BoxUsage
u'0.0055590278'
>>>
>>>
```

Let's create another domain and compare the BoxUsage values for each create operation.

```
>>> new_domain = sdb_connection.create_domain('tuning_2')
>>> new_domain.BoxUsage
u'0.0055590278'
>>>
>>>
```

The values are exactly the same. SimpleDB BoxUsage values seem to vary only for select operations, and are quite consistent for the domain-related operations. Let us try the other operations such as getting its metadata.

```
>>> metadata = new_domain.get_metadata()
>>>
>>> metadata.BoxUsage
u'0.0000071759'
>>>
```

Boto has a very nice method available on the connection object that gives you the cumulative BoxUsage value for all calls made to SimpleDB using that specific connection object. You can either print out the cumulative BoxUsage value or a dollar value for the BoxUsage.

```
>>>
>>> sdb_connection.print_usage()
Total Usage: 0.005559 compute seconds
Approximate Cost: $0.000778
>>>
>>> sdb_connection.get_usage()
0.0055590277999999996
```

```
>>>

>>>
```

When you delete a domain, boto returns only the status for the operation, but it is quite simple to get the BoxUsage for the delete operation using the cumulative values we looked at previously.

```
>>>
>>> current_usage = sdb_connection.get_usage()
>>>
>>> sdb_connection.delete_domain('tuning')
True
>>> usage = sdb_connection.get_usage()
>>>
>>> current_usage - usage
-0.0055590277999999996
>>> print current_usage
0.0055590278
>>>
>>> print usage
0.0111180556
>>> usage - current_usage
0.0055590277999999996
>>>
```

Partitioning

SimpleDB is designed to provide a maximum of 100 domains per account and each domain is limited to a maximum domain data size of 10 GB. There is always the possibility that the size limitation of 10 GB will be a limiting factor when your dataset needs to be larger. In such cases, SimpleDB gives you the ability to create multiple domains. This will of course mean that data will need to be partitioned among the multiple domains so that each dataset in a domain is under the 10 GB size limit.

Your dataset might naturally partition along some dimension. For example, let us assume that our songs domain is hitting the limit of 10 GB. We could partition our domain into multiple domains, each dedicated to a specific genre. However, this will add complexity to our application as currently SimpleDB domain queries cannot be made across domains. Any partitioning of the data means that we will need to make select queries for each domain and then aggregate the results in the application layer.

Performance is the most common reason to partition your data. Multiple domains increase the potential throughput. Each domain is limited to about 50 to 100 puts per second. Split a domain into 4 and you increase throughput to 200 to 400 puts per second. This is the key for large scaling applications.

Another reason for partitioning is that our queries start hitting the timeout limit due to the large dataset. In this case, we can make queries against the smaller multiple domains and aggregate the queries.

> If you require additional domains above the limit of 100, you can request an increase in the limit for your account at `http://aws.amazon.com/contact-us/simpledb-limit-request/`.

Summary

In this chapter, we discussed the BoxUsage of different SimpleDB queries and the usage costs, along with viewing the usage activity reports. In the next chapter, we are going to look at using caching along with SimpleDB.

9
Caching

SimpleDB requests can add up very quickly if you are not careful with the design of your application. In this chapter, we will consider one simple strategy for avoiding excessive SimpleDB requests: using a cache to store the data locally. The cache that we will be using to accomplish this is called **memcached**. While memcached supports PHP, we will use Cache_Lite in some samples. Cache_Lite is similar in concept but a lighter-weight API. It stores the cached data in temporary files.

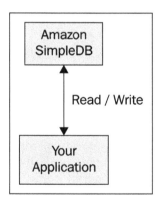

Caching

Caching can help alleviate both the issue of making extra requests to SimpleDB and the issue with eventual consistency. We discussed the principle of eventual consistency in the earlier chapters, and it is one of the main principles behind the design of SimpleDB. However, the possibility that things may not be consistent immediately after you make some change to your SimpleDB data can throw things out of whack for your own application. If you are aware that this can happen, you can take it into consideration when designing your SimpleDB-based application and leverage caching to help alleviate it.

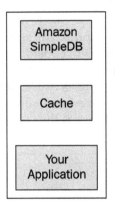

Memcached

The most popular solution used for caching these days is called **memcached**. It is an open source project originally developed by Danga Interactive and used for their LiveJournal website. Since then, it has been used all over the world to improve the performance and scalability characteristics of applications and web applications. Some of the most heavily used applications on the Internet leverage memcached, such as these:

- Facebook
- Twitter
- Digg
- LiveJournal

- Flickr
- Youtube
- Wordpress
- CraigsList

Memcached consists of two core components, a memcached server and a memcached client. The clients are available in various languages allowing you to use memcached from Ruby, Java, Python, PHP, C#, C++, and many other programming languages.

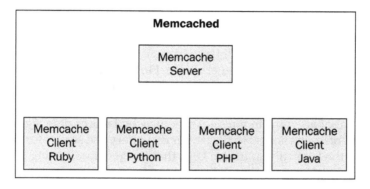

Memcached is a high-performance, distributed memory object caching system, generic in nature, but intended for use in speeding up dynamic web applications by alleviating database load.

The latest list of client libraries for memcached can be found at `http://code.google.com/p/memcached/wiki/Clients`. At the most basic level, memcached can be considered a simple memory cache that can be deployed anywhere and accessed from anywhere over a network. The beauty of memcached is that it is great for storing data using a key and then retrieving that data back using the key. Memcached utilizes highly efficient, non-blocking networking libraries and as a result is very, very fast and high performing. There are three things that you will almost always do when using memcached at a high level:

- Write values using keys and expiry times
- Get values using keys
- Be able to expire keys from the system

Memcached and security

Memcached is a memory cache and does not have any built-in security features to prevent access to it. It is highly recommended that you only run memcached inside your firewall where you can restrict access to the server that runs it.

Here are some measures that you can take to improve and harden the security when using memcached:

- Deploy memcached behind your firewall and only allow machines from within a trusted network to access the cache.

- Encrypt any data that you store in memcached. This will increase the processing times, as you will have to encrypt data before you store it and then decrypt it on retrieval every time. However, if you are storing sensitive information, the additional processing overhead is well worth it to secure the information.

- Use keys that are hard to guess. As memcached stores data signed keys, anyone who gains access to the server can query the server for data by guessing the keys. If you utilize keys that are generated using a hash algorithm on some simple strings, it will be next to impossible for anyone to just guess the key. This will again add a little overhead due to the key generation, but depending on your application, it may be well worth the effort.

Installing memcached

You can usually install memcached for the Linux distribution of your choice by using the package system used by that version of Linux—**RPM** for **Red Hat**-based Linux systems or **APT** for **Debian**-based Linux systems. This will usually get you the latest compatible version for that distribution. However, memcached is a fast-evolving project, and they are constantly improving it or adding security bug fixes. It is also a very widely used project, so the community is constantly providing patches to memcached.

 The best way to ensure that you are using the latest stable version is to get the source yourself and compile and install it. This is a pretty straightforward process and follows standard Linux installation procedures.

The latest version of memcached is always available at `http://memcached.org/`. At the time of writing this chapter, the latest version of memcached is 1.4.4.

```
# cd /usr/local/src
```

```
# wget http://memcached.googlecode.com/files/memcached-1.4.4.tar.gz
```

```
# tar zxvf memcached-1.4.4.tar.gz
```

```
# cd memcached-1.4.4
```

```
# ./configure
```

```
# make && make install
```

You can test that it is installed correctly by running memcached and printing out its help options.

```
# memcached -h
memcached 1.4.4
-p <num>       TCP port number to listen on (default: 11211)
-U <num>       UDP port number to listen on (default: 11211, 0 is off)
-s <file>      UNIX socket path to listen on (disables network support)
-a <mask>      access mask for UNIX socket, in octal (default: 0700)
-l <ip_addr>   interface to listen on (default: INADDR_ANY, all addresses)
-d             run as a daemon
-r             maximize core file limit
-u <username>  assume identity of <username> (only when run as root)
-m <num>       max memory to use for items in megabytes (default: 64 MB)
-M             return error on memory exhausted (rather than removing
items)
-c <num>       max simultaneous connections (default: 1024)
-k             lock down all paged memory.  Note that there is a
               limit on how much memory you may lock.  Trying to
               allocate more than that would fail, so be sure you
               set the limit correctly for the user you started
               the daemon with (not for -u <username> user;
               under sh this is done with 'ulimit -S -l NUM_KB').
-v             verbose (print errors/warnings while in event loop)
-vv            very verbose (also print client commands/reponses)
-vvv           extremely verbose (also print internal state transitions)
```

```
-h                print this help and exit
-i                print memcached and libevent license
-P <file>         save PID in <file>, only used with -d option
-f <factor>       chunk size growth factor (default: 1.25)
-n <bytes>        minimum space allocated for key+value+flags (default: 48)
-L                Try to use large memory pages (if available). Increasing
                  the memory page size could reduce the number of TLB misses
                  and improve the performance. In order to get large pages
                  from the OS, memcached will allocate the total item-cache
                  in one large chunk.
-D <char>         Use <char> as the delimiter between key prefixes and IDs.
                  This is used for per-prefix stats reporting. The default is
                  ":" (colon). If this option is specified, stats collection
                  is turned on automatically; if not, then it may be turned
on
                  by sending the "stats detail on" command to the server.
-t <num>          number of threads to use (default: 4)
-R                Maximum number of requests per event, limits the number of
                  requests process for a given connection to prevent
                  starvation (default: 20)
-C                Disable use of CAS
-b                Set the backlog queue limit (default: 1024)
-B                Binding protocol - one of ascii, binary, or auto (default)
-I                Override the size of each slab page. Adjusts max item size
                  (default: 1mb, min: 1k, max: 128m)
```

Now you have memcached installed. Please take a look at all of the different options that are available for configuring it. The most common things that you will want to modify or consider are:

- Memcached by default runs and listens on port number 11211. You may want to change this port to a different number if you like.

- You need to specify if you want to run it as a daemon.

Now we are going to run memcached as a daemon listening on port 12312, so we can connect to it and start using it for caching our data.

```
memcached -p 12312 -d
```

Installing memcached client

We need a client library to connect to the memcached server and store and retrieve data. In this section we will install memcached clients for Java, PHP, and Python.

Memcached client in Java

The best available client in Java is named `java_memcached`, and was created by Greg Whalin. It is currently hosted on GitHub at `http://github.com/gwhalin/Memcached-Java-Client`. Download the latest version of this library from `http://github.com/gwhalin/Memcached-Java-Client/downloads`. The most current version at the time of writing this chapter is 2.5.0. Unzip the distribution to the directory of choice. Copy the JAR file named `java_memcached-release_2.5.0.jar` to a folder that is on your classpath. You are now ready to start using this library to interact with our memcached server.

Memcached client in PHP

There are two available clients in PHP: `pecl/memcache` (`http://pecl.php.net/package/memcache`) and `pecl/memcached` (`http://pecl.php.net/package/memcached`). The first, `pecl/memcache`, has been around since 2004 and is the most popular. The second, `pecl/memcached`, has only been available since Jan 2009 but has more features.

Both packages are built on **PHP Extension Community Library (PECL)**, which is not installed in PHP by default.

Memcached client in Python

There are multiple libraries available for Python, but we will use the `python-memcached` library that is available from `http://www.tummy.com/Community/software/python-memcached/`. At the time of writing this chapter, the version of `python-memcached` is 1.45. Download and install the package for your version of Python.

```
# wget ftp://ftp.tummy.com/pub/python-memcached/python-memcached-1.45.tar.gz

# tar zxvf python-memcached-1.45.tar.gz

# cd python-memcached-1.45

# sudo python setup.py install
```

Run a quick test to make sure that it was installed correctly. Open up a Python console session and import the memcached library and there should not be any import errors.

```
# python
Python 2.5.1 (r251:54863, Feb  6 2009, 19:02:12)
[GCC 4.0.1 (Apple Inc. build 5465)] on darwin
Type "help", "copyright", "credits" or "license" for more information.
>>>
>>> import memcache
>>>
```

We now have the Python memcached client library installed and configured.

Storing and retrieving data from memcached

It is quite simple to use the memcached client. In this section we will store and retrieve data from the memcached server and get a feel for the API.

Storing and retrieving data from memcached in Java

The first thing we need to do before retrieving data is to actually create a connection to the memcached server. A static pool of servers is used by the client. You can of course specify more than one memcached server for the pool. Once we have a connection object, it can be used for all of the interaction with the server, and for setting and retrieving keys and their associated values. Here is a simple class that shows how we would do this in Java:

```java
package simpledbbook;

import com.danga.MemCached.MemCachedClient;
import com.danga.MemCached.SockIOPool;
import java.util.Date;

public class MemcacheClientSdbBook {
    // A static pool of memcache servers for the client
    static {
        String[] serverList = {"localhost:11211"};
        SockIOPool pool = SockIOPool.getInstance();
        pool.setServers(serverList);
```

```
        pool.initialize();
    }

    public static void main(String[] args) {
        MemCachedClient mc = new MemCachedClient();
        String key = "any_key";
        System.out.println(mc.get(key));

        // Set and get the keys
        mc.set(key, "Java is cool!");
        System.out.println(mc.get(key));

        // If you specify the same key name, it will overwrite the
existing value
        mc.set(key, "Java is very cool!");
        System.out.println(mc.get(key));

        // This key will expire after 30 seconds
        mc.set(key, "Java is very cool!", new Date(System.
currentTimeMillis() + 30000));
    }
}
```

Storing and retrieving data from memcached in PHP

Once a connection is made to memcached, the Select syntax is formed and memcached is checked for that syntax as the key to see if the query was done. If so, those results are returned; if not, then the actual Select to the SimpleDB database is done and the results are stored in memcached as well as returned.

```
// query
$sql = "select * from songs where itemName() = '112222222'";

// create an index key for memcache
$key = md5('select'.$sql);

//lookup value in memcache
$result = $memcache->get($key);

//check if we got something back
if($result == null) {
  //fetch from database
  $rest = $sdb->select($domain,$sql);
  if ($rest) {
    $result = $rest;
    //store in memcache
    $memcache->set($key,$result,0,3600);
```

```
    }
  }
  // $results has the cached copy or the live query
```

Storing and retrieving data from memcached in Python

The first thing we will need to do is actually create a connection to our local memcached server from Python.

```
>>>
>>> mc = memcache.Client(['127.0.0.1:12312'])
>>>
```

We do not yet have any data stored, so trying to retrieve a non-existent key will return nothing.

```
>>>
>>> val = mc.get("any_key")
>>>
>>> print val
None
>>>
```

Let us store and retrieve data from the cache.

```
>>>
>>> mc.set("my_key", "Python is cool!")
True
>>>
>>> val = mc.get("my_key")
>>>
>>> print val
Python is cool!
>>>
```

If you store an object into the cache with an existing key, it will overwrite the previously stored object.

```
>>> mc.set("my_key", "Python is very cool!", 30)
True
>>> val = mc.get("my_key")
```

```
>>>
>>> print val
Python is very cool!
>>>
```

You can also specify an expiration time when you store the data into the cache. After 30 seconds, this value will be automatically purged from the cache by the memcached server.

```
>>>
>>> mc.set("my_key", "Python is cool!", 30)
True
```

We now have the memcached server installed and running as a daemon and also have a Java, PHP, or a Python client library installed that we can use for storing and retrieving data in our memcached server. In the next section, we will start looking at how we can utilize memcached to alleviate the burden on SimpleDB and speed up our data retrieval process by leveraging the cache.

Cache_Lite

Cache_Lite is a light-weight cache system. Cache_Lite uses file locking and anti-corruption tests. Another key advantage is that it installs from the **PHP Extensions and Applications Repository (PEAR)**. On cPanel Linux servers, Cache_Lite can be installed from the PHP PEAR Package's icon from http://pear.php.net/package/Cache_Lite. Just click and it is ready to use. Cache_Lite is optimized for high-traffic websites so it is really fast and safe because it uses file locking and/or anti-corruption tests. You can find documentation from http://pear.php.net/manual/en/package.caching.cache-lite.php.

Logic flow for using caching with SimpleDB

Here is the flow of logic when we use memcached with SimpleDB:

1. When you need to retrieve data from SimpleDB, first query memcached server to see if the data is currently available in the cache.

2. If the data is in the cache, then simply return the data, and do not make a request to SimpleDB.

3. If the data is not in the cache, retrieve it from SimpleDB, and store it in the cache before returning the results back, so it is available next time you need it in the cache.

4. If you are updating the data, all you have to do is update SimpleDB and also delete the data from the cache. This will ensure that the next request from the data will get the latest information from SimpleDB and not outdated information from the cache. You can also just update the cache with the latest data that you have, thus alleviating any issue with eventual consistency, returning stale data when you turn around and make a request immediately.

5. If you have data that automatically goes stale after a fixed period of time, you can always have a background process or job that periodically clears the cache and puts the latest information into the cache. You can also tell memcached server to expire data and remove it from the cache automatically by specifying the amount of time the data needs to be in the cache when storing it.

Using memcached with SimpleDB in Java

The usage of **memcached** client is quite simple, as we have seen in the previous section. Now we are going to integrate the client into a simple class that interacts with SimpleDB, so you can see the advantages brought to the table by **memcached**. The class listed next is just an example and it always queries the **memcached** server for data before it goes and retrieves it from SimpleDB. You can use any string value as the key for storage. We will use the name of the item as the key for this example.

```
package simpledbbook;

import com.danga.MemCached.MemCachedClient;
import com.danga.MemCached.SockIOPool;
import com.xerox.amazonws.sdb.Domain;
import com.xerox.amazonws.sdb.ItemAttribute;
import com.xerox.amazonws.sdb.QueryWithAttributesResult;
import com.xerox.amazonws.sdb.SDBException;
import com.xerox.amazonws.sdb.SimpleDB;
import java.math.BigInteger;
import java.security.MessageDigest;
import java.security.NoSuchAlgorithmException;
import java.util.ArrayList;
import java.util.Date;
import java.util.List;
import java.util.Map;

public class MemcacheSdbSongs {
    private static MemCachedClient mc = null;
```

```
private static SimpleDB sdb = null;

// Initialize the memcache client and our SDB connection
static {
    String[] serverList = {"localhost:11211"};
    SockIOPool pool = SockIOPool.getInstance();
    pool.setServers(serverList);
    pool.initialize();
    mc = new MemCachedClient();
    sdb = new SimpleDB(awsAccessId, awsSecretKey, true);
}

private static String
  createHashedKeyFromQueryString(String query) {
    try {
        MessageDigest md5 = MessageDigest.getInstance("MD5");
        md5.update(query.getBytes());
        BigInteger hash = new BigInteger(1, md5.digest());
        return hash.toString(16);
    } catch (NoSuchAlgorithmException ex) {
        System.out.println(ex.getMessage());
        return "";
    }
}

public static List<Map<String, List<ItemAttribute>>>
    selectFromSdb(String domainName, String queryString,
    Date expirationTime) {
    // Check if the key exists in the cache
    String cacheKey =
        createHashedKeyFromQueryString(queryString);
    List<Map<String, List<ItemAttribute>>>
        fromCache = (List<Map<String, List<ItemAttribute>>>)
        mc.get(cacheKey);
    if (fromCache == null) {
        System.out.println("++++ Query not found in cache
            . Retrieving from SimpleDB.");
        try {
            Domain domain = sdb.getDomain(domainName);
            List<Map<String, List<ItemAttribute>>>
                queryitems = new ArrayList<Map<String,
                            List<ItemAttribute>>>();
            String nextToken = null;
            do {
                QueryWithAttributesResult queryResults = domain
                    .selectItems(queryString, nextToken);
```

```
                    Map<String, List<ItemAttribute>> items =
                        queryResults.getItems();
                    queryitems.add(items);
                    nextToken = queryResults.getNextToken();
                } while (nextToken != null && !nextToken
                    .trim().equals(""));
                mc.set(cacheKey, queryitems);
                fromCache = queryitems;
            } catch (SDBException ex) {
                System.out.println(ex.getMessage());
            }
        } else {
            System.out.println("**** Query found in cache");
        }

        return fromCache;
    }

    public static void main(String[] args) {
        String queryString = "SELECT * FROM `songs`
                             WHERE `Year` = '1980'";
        List<Map<String, List<ItemAttribute>>>
            queryItems = selectFromSdb("songs", queryString,
            new Date(System.currentTimeMillis() + 60000));
        for (Map<String, List<ItemAttribute>> items : queryItems) {
            for (String id : items.keySet()) {
                System.out.println("Item : " + id);
                for (ItemAttribute attr : items.get(id)) {
                    System.out.println("    " + attr.getName()
                        + " = " + attr.getValue());
                }
            }
        }
    }
}
```

The first time you run a query, it will not find the items in the cache, so it will go and retrieve them from SimpleDB. So you will see the following printed out to the console:

```
++++ Query not found in cache. Retrieving from SimpleDB.
Item : 5656600009
     Year = 1980
     Song = Acapulco
     Rating = *
     Rating = Avoid
```

```
Rating = 1 star
Genre = Soundtrack
Artist = Neil Diamond
```

The next time you run the query, it should find the items in the cache.

```
**** Query found in cache
Item : 5656600009
    Year = 1980
    Song = Acapulco
    Rating = *
    Rating = Avoid
    Rating = 1 star
    Genre = Soundtrack
    Artist = Neil Diamond
```

One important thing to keep in mind is that the memcached server has a limit of 1 MB for the size of each item stored in it. If your data needs to be larger than that limit, you should look at the various command-line options that can be provided when starting your server.

Using Cache_Lite with SimpleDB in PHP

There are two samples of Cache_Lite with PHP. First is `cachetest.php`. This program just uses Cache_Lite calls to store a value and retrieve it. This program is useful to ensure your installation of Cache_Lite is working.

File: `cachetest.php`

```php
require_once('Cache/Lite.php');
// Set a id for this cache
$id = "select * from songs where itemName() = '112222222'";
// Set a few options
$options = array(
    'cacheDir' => '/tmp/',
    'lifeTime' => 3600
);
// Create a Cache_Lite object
$Cache_Lite = new Cache_Lite($options);
if ($cc) {
  echo("<p><b>Removing from Cache : </b>" . $id . "<p>");
  $Cache_Lite->remove($id, "default"); // clear cache first
```

```
    }
    // Test if there is a valid cache for this id
    if ($data = $Cache_Lite->get($id, "default")) {
        // Content is in $data
        echo("<b>Cache Data : </b>" . $data . "<br>Key : "
            . $id.  "<p>");
    } else { // No valid cache found
      // Put in $data datas to put in cache
      $newdata = "Results from SimpleDB";
      $Cache_Lite->save($newdata, $id, "default");
      echo("<b>Saving in Cache : </b>" . $data. "<br>Key : " . $id .
    "<p>");
    }
```

This program demonstrates the basics of Cache_Lite. This program takes an ID and calls the cache to try fetching it. If the fetch fails then a value is stored in the cache. If the clearcache checkbox is checked then the cache is first cleared of that value so that the actual value will need to be fetched.

File: selectcachetest.php

```php
<?php
$domain = "songs";
if (!empty($_POST["sql"])) {
  // if a value is passed from the key input field save it
    $sql = $_POST["sql"];
} else {
    $sql = "";
}
$sql = stripslashes($sql);  // remove PHP escaping
if (!empty($_POST["domain"])) {
  // if a value is passed from the key input field save it
    $domain = $_POST["domain"];
} else {
$domain = "songs";
}
$domain = stripslashes($domain);  // remove PHP escaping
$clearcache = $_POST["clearcache"];
if ($clearcache=="Yes") {
    $cc = true;
} else {
    $cc = false;
}
?>
```

This part of the program sets up variables $domain, $sql, and $cc, where $domain has the name of the domain, $sql has the SQL statement to execute, and $cc has the Boolean value as to whether to clear the cache before executing the Select.

In the next part, the user interface is set up asking for input for the variables.

```
<FORM ACTION="selectcachetest.php" METHOD=post>
<textarea name="sql" cols=60><?php echo($sql); ?></textarea> SQL<br>
<input type=text name="domain" size=40
       value="<?php echo $domain; ?>"> Domain<br>
<input type="checkbox" name="clearcache" value="Yes" />
    Clear this value from cache first<br>
<INPUT TYPE=submit VALUE="Run SQL">
</FORM>
```

Now the Select can be performed. First the cache and the SDB APIs are initialized. If Clearcache is true, then the cache is cleared. Now try retrieving the data from the cache using the SQL as the key. Cache_Lite only stores strings. The data returned from the SDB API is an array, so serialize and unserialize are used to convert from an array to a string. If the data is found in the cache, it is converted back to an array with unserialize. If the data is not in the cache, SimpleDB is called. Before returning the data array, a copy is serialized and stored in the cache.

```php
<?php
// Uses Cache_Lite - http://pear.php.net/package/Cache_Lite
// Include the package
require_once('Cache/Lite.php');
// Set a few options
$options = array(
    'cacheDir' => '/tmp/',
    'lifeTime' => 3600
);
if (!class_exists('SimpleDB')) require_once('sdb.php');
$sdb = new SimpleDB(awsAccessKey, awsSecretKey); // create connection
if (!empty($sql)) {
    // Create a Cache_Lite object
    $Cache_Lite = new Cache_Lite($options);
    if ($cc) {
        echo("<p><b>Removing from Cache : </b>" . $sql . "<p>");
        $Cache_Lite->remove($sql, $domain); // clear cache first
    }
    // Test if there is a valid cache for this id
    if ($data = $Cache_Lite->get($sql, $domain)) {
```

```
            $rest = unserialize($data);
            // Content is in $data
            echo("<p><b>Retrieving from Cache : </b>" . $sql . "<p>");
        } else { // No valid cache found
            $rest = $sdb->select($domain,$sql);
            $data = serialize($rest);

            // Put in $data datas to put in cache
            $Cache_Lite->save($data, $sql, $domain);

            echo("<p><b>Saving in Cache : </b>" . $sql . "<p>");
        }
        echo(SimpleDB::dumpResults($rest));
        if ($sdb->BoxUsage) {
            echo("RequestId: ".$sdb->RequestId."<br>");
            echo("BoxUsage: ".$sdb->BoxUsage." = "
                . SimpleDB::displayUsage($sdb->BoxUsage)."<br>");
            echo("NextToken: <pre>".$sdb->NextToken."</pre><br>");
        }
        if ($sdb->ErrorCode) {
            echo("Listing FAILED<br>");
            echo("ErrorCode: ".$sdb->ErrorCode."<p>");
        }
    }
?>
```

The results are then dumped to the screen. In the sample, the last routine displays the SimpleDB BoxUsage or error code if there is one. As these are not returned in the array, they would also have not been stored in the cache.

In a real implementation, the cache would be cleared when a put was performed on a record. Caching would be most useful using getAttributes, as it would be easy to control. The key is the item name. The item attributes/values are cached. If the item is updated with a put, then the cache is cleared using the same key, the item name.

The key to performance would be to integrate the cache in the getAttributes call to store the original XML string from SimpleDB, rather than the serializing and unserializing the results array. The XML approach would call none of this overhead.

Rich Helms: "I added notes in the source code to the putAttributes and getAttributes functions on where hooks into caching would be added".

Using memcached with SimpleDB in Python

Listed below is a simple Python class saved in a file named `memcached_wrapper.py` that wraps the memcached API:

```python
import memcache
"""
Memcached client wrapper class
"""
class MemcachedWrapper():
    """Memcached client Wrapper"""
    mchost = ""
    mcserver  = ""
    def __init__(self, server="127.0.0.1", port="11211"):
        self.mchost = "%s:%s" % (server, port)
        self.mcserver  = memcache.Client([self.mchost])
    def set(self, key, value, expiry=600):
        """
        Store a value in the memcached server.
        """
        self.mcserver.set(key, value, expiry)
    def get(self, key):
        """
        Retrieve a value from the memcached server.
        """
        return self.mcserver.get(key)
    def delete(self, key):
        """
        Delete a value from the memcached server.
        """
        self.mcserver.delete(key)
```

Using this class with SimpleDB is quite simple. We will create a class that will encapsulate the logic for using memcached with SimpleDB. This class is intentionally simple to clarify the concepts involved without being bogged down with too much detail.

```python
import boto
import hashlib
from memcached_wrapper import MemcachedWrapper
"""
Using Memcached with SimpleDB domain Songs
"""
class SDBMemcache():
```

```
    """This will use your AWS keys that are exported as
    environment variables"""
    sdbconn = boto.connect_sdb()
    mcserver = ""

    def __init__(self, server="127.0.0.1", port="11211"):
        self.mcserver   = MemcachedWrapper(server, port)

    def select_from_sdb(self, domain_name, query, expiry=600):
        """
        Retrieve from SDB. Check if it exists in the
        memcached server first. If it doesn't exist in the
        cache, save it to the cache by hashing the query as
        the key
        """
        hasher = hashlib.md5()
        hasher.update(query)
        hashkey_for_query = hasher.hexdigest()
        in_cache = self.mcserver.get(hashkey_for_query)
        if in_cache:
            print '**** Query found in cache'
            return in_cache
        else:
            print '++++ Query not found in cache. Retrieving from
SimpleDB.'
            query_rs = self.sdbconn.select(domain_name, query)
            store_in_cache = []
            for item in query_rs:
                store_in_cache.append({item.name : item.values()})
            self.mcserver.set(hashkey_for_query, store_in_cache, 600)
            return store_in_cache
```

We use Python's **hashlib** module to calculate a digest value for the query and use that value as our key in the memcached server. If it does not exist, we go retrieve it from SimpleDB or else we return it immediately from our cache.

Let us now run a query against SimpleDB and see our cache in action.

```
>>>
>>> from sdb_memcache import SDBMemcache
>>>
>>> sdb_mc = SDBMemcache("127.0.0.1","12312")
>>>
>>> sdb_mc.select_from_sdb("songs", "Select * from songs WHERE `Year` =
'2002'")
```

```
++++ Query not found in cache. Retrieving from SimpleDB.

[{u'112222222': [[u'****', u'Excellent', u'4 stars'], u'My Way', u'b194a
34e3340bc1e7df4e8b92a6b95d3', u'Frank Sinatra', u'My Way.mp3', u'2002',
u'Easy Listening'}]
>>>
```

As this is the first time that we ran this query, it does not exist in the cache so we have to go retrieve it from SimpleDB. If you run this same query again within 10 minutes, which is the expiry time that we have set for the cache, you should get it from the cache without another call to SimpleDB.

```
>>>

>>> sdb_mc.select_from_sdb("songs", "Select * from songs WHERE `Year` =
'2002'")

**** Query found in cache

[{u'112222222': [[u'****', u'Excellent', u'4 stars'], u'My Way', u'b194a
34e3340bc1e7df4e8b92a6b95d3', u'Frank Sinatra', u'My Way.mp3', u'2002',
u'Easy Listening'}]
>>>
```

In this section we looked at several different ways to use SimpleDB and memcached together. You can layer this with your specific requirements and build up a more complex caching strategy for use with SimpleDB. You can experiment with other strategies and find one that matches your application requirements.

Summary

In this chapter, we discussed memcached and Cache_Lite and their use for caching. We also explored a way we can use memcached with SimpleDB to avoid making unnecessary requests to SimpleDB, that is, by using libraries in Java, PHP, and Python. In the next chapter, we are going to look at another way to speed up retrieval from SimpleDB by using parallel queries and multi-threading.

10
Parallel Processing

So far, all our queries and interaction with SimpleDB have been the single-threaded way. The data that we have been inserting has not really needed anything else. However, one of the things that really sets it apart is its support for concurrency and parallel operations. This support is what truly makes it a scalable database. In this chapter, we will explore how to run parallel operations against SimpleDB using boto.

- Discuss the concept of BatchPutAttributes and explore its usage with code samples in Java, PHP, and Python
- Parallelize our SimpleDB requests with examples in Java, PHP, and Python

BatchPutAttributes

The original release of SimpleDB only provided the ability to update or save attributes for a single item per call. As you can imagine, this can cause major performance issues if you had updated several items and their attributes, as you would have to make one SimpleDB call for each item. This may not seem like such a big deal, but once the number of items to be updated starts going above 100, this becomes very significant. SimpleDB released support for insert or update of multiple items in the form of BatchPutAttributes. This is a nice way to perform multiple PutAttribute operations in a single call, saving unnecessary round trips and network and HTTP response/request latencies to the SimpleDB server.

BatchPutAttributes in Java

In this section, we will create a Java class that will update attributes for multiple items by making a single call to SimpleDB. We will accomplish that by using the support for BatchPutAttributes provided by **Typica**. The following code runs a query against SimpleDB and prints the results from the query. Then we update attributes for both of these items, and run another query and print the results to show that the update was completed successfully.

```java
package simpledbbook;

import com.xerox.amazonws.sdb.Domain;
import com.xerox.amazonws.sdb.ItemAttribute;
import com.xerox.amazonws.sdb.QueryWithAttributesResult;
import com.xerox.amazonws.sdb.SDBException;
import com.xerox.amazonws.sdb.SimpleDB;
import java.util.ArrayList;
import java.util.HashMap;
import java.util.List;
import java.util.Map;

public class BatchPutSongAttributes {
    public static void main(String[] args) {
        SimpleDB sdb = new SimpleDB(awsAccessId, awsSecretKey, true);
        try {
            Domain domain = sdb.getDomain("songs");
            String queryString = "SELECT * FROM `songs`
                WHERE `Song`='My Way' OR `Song`='Transmission'";
            System.out.println("Items before batch update
                ************");
            String nextToken = null;
            do {
                QueryWithAttributesResult queryResults = domain
                    .selectItems(queryString, nextToken);
                Map<String, List<ItemAttribute>> items = queryResults
                    .getItems();
                for (String id : items.keySet()) {
                    System.out.println("Item : " + id);
                    for (ItemAttribute attr : items.get(id)) {
                        System.out.println(attr.getName() + " = "
                            + attr.getValue());
                    }
                }
                nextToken = queryResults.getNextToken();
            } while (nextToken != null &&
                !nextToken.trim().equals(""));
```

```
        Map<String, List<ItemAttribute>> multipleItems
            = new HashMap<String, List<ItemAttribute>>();

        List<ItemAttribute> list = new
            ArrayList<ItemAttribute>();
        list.add(new ItemAttribute("Year", "2009", true));
        multipleItems.put("112222222", list);

        list = new ArrayList<ItemAttribute>();
        list.add(new ItemAttribute("Genre", "Rock", true));
        multipleItems.put("6767969119", list);

        domain.batchPutAttributes(multipleItems);

        long sleeptime = 5000L;
        System.out.println("Sleeping for 5 seconds after the
            update. Ah! Eventual Consistency ...");
        try {
            Thread.sleep(sleeptime);
        } catch (InterruptedException e) {
            e.printStackTrace();
        }

        System.out.println("Items after batch update
            ************");
        do {
            QueryWithAttributesResult queryResults
                = domain.selectItems(queryString, nextToken);
            Map<String, List<ItemAttribute>> items = queryResults
                .getItems();
            for (String id : items.keySet()) {
                System.out.println("Item : " + id);
                for (ItemAttribute attr : items.get(id)) {
                    System.out.println(attr.getName() + " = "
                    + attr.getValue());
                }
            }
            nextToken = queryResults.getNextToken();
        } while (nextToken != null &&
            !nextToken.trim().equals(""));
    } catch (SDBException ex) {
        System.out.println(ex.getMessage());
    }
  }
}
```

Here is the output from running this sample. The first part of the console output shows the attribute values before the change, and the later part of the output displays the changed attribute values as a result of our call to BatchPutAttributes.

```
Items before batch update ************
Item : 112222222
Year = 2002
Year = 2009
Song = My Way
Rating = 4 stars
Rating = ****
Rating = Excellent
Genre = Easy Listening
Artist = Frank Sinatra
Item : 6767969119
Year = 1981
Song = Transmission
Rating = *****
Rating = Excellent
Genre = Alternative
Genre = Rock
Genre = Rocket
Artist = Joy Division

Sleeping for 5 seconds after the update. Ah! Eventual Consistency ...

Items after batch update ************
Item : 112222222
Year = 2009
Song = My Way
Rating = 4 stars
Rating = Excellent
Rating = ****
Genre = Easy Listening
Artist = Frank Sinatra
Item : 6767969119
Year = 1981
Song = Transmission
Rating = Excellent
Rating = *****
Genre = Rock
Artist = Joy Division
```

BatchPutAttributes in PHP

Let's start with a review of putting a single item with `putAttributes`.

```
$sdb = new SimpleDB(awsAccessKey, awsSecretKey); // create connection

$domain = "car-s";

$item_name = "car1";

$putAttributesRequest["make"] = array("value" => "Acura");
$putAttributesRequest["color"] =
    array("value" => array("Black","Red"));
$putAttributesRequest["desc"] =
    array("value" => "Sedan", "replace" => "true");
  // replace existing value

$rest = $sdb->
    putAttributes($domain,$item_name,$putAttributesRequest);

if ($rest) {
    echo("Item $item_name created");
    echo("RequestId: ".$sdb->RequestId."<br>");
    echo("BoxUsage: ".$sdb->BoxUsage." = " .
SimpleDB::displayUsage($sdb->BoxUsage)."<br>");
} else {
    echo("Item $item_name FAILED<br>");
    echo("ErrorCode: ".$sdb->ErrorCode."<p>");
}
```

There are three examples of adding an attribute pair:

- `make` is a simple pair with one value
- `color` adds an array or values
- `desc` is set to replace the value if there is one

After that `putAttributes` is called, passing the domain and the array of values. To add another item, the item name will be set, the array will be cleared, the new values will be added, and then another call will be made. In `batchPutAttributes` we will do the same thing but build one array with the items and attribute/value pairs in it. Then make one call with `batchPutAttributes`.

```
$sdb = new SimpleDB(awsAccessKey, awsSecretKey);

$domain = "car-s";

$putAttributesRequest = array();

$item_name = "car1";
$putAttributesRequest["make"] = array("value" => "Acura"); // Single
```

```
$putAttributesRequest["color"] = array("value" =>
    array("Black","Red")); // Multiple
$bulkAttr[$item_name] = array("name" => "$item_name", "attributes" =>
    $putAttributesRequest);

$item_name = "car2";
unset($putAttributesRequest);   // clear array
$putAttributesRequest["make"] = array("value" => "BMW");
$putAttributesRequest["year"] = array("value" => "2008");
$bulkAttr[$item_name] = array("name" => "$item_name", "attributes" =>
    $putAttributesRequest);

$item_name = "car3";
unset($putAttributesRequest);   // clear array
$putAttributesRequest["make"] = array("value" => "Lexus"); // Single
$putAttributesRequest["color"] = array("value" =>
    array("Blue","Red")); // Multiple
$putAttributesRequest["year"] = array("value" => "2008");
$putAttributesRequest["desc"] = array("value" => "Sedan", "replace"
    => "true"); // Replace
$bulkAttr[$item_name] = array("name" => "$item_name",
    "attributes" => $putAttributesRequest);

if ($sdb->batchPutAttributes($domain,$bulkAttr)) {
    echo("Items created<br>");
    echo("RequestId: ".$sdb->RequestId."<br>");
    echo("BoxUsage: ".$sdb->BoxUsage." = "
        . SimpleDB::displayUsage($sdb->BoxUsage)."<br>");
} else {
    echo("Items FAILED<br>");
    echo("ErrorCode: ".$sdb->ErrorCode."<p>");
}
```

Now in addition to the item name and attribute array, we create an array called
bulkAttr which is the holder for the multiple items, attributes, or values. Note the
maximum number of items you can send in one call is 25.

BatchPutAttributes in Python

Boto provides full support for this operation. This operation can be invoked on a boto domain object by specifying a dictionary of items to be updated. The keys of this dictionary are names of these items while the values for the keys are again dictionaries, each of which contains the attribute name/values that are to be updated. You can also specify if the existing values are to be replaced or if these attribute values are to be added to the existing ones. The default option is to replace the existing attribute values with the provided values. The default option in SimpleDB is to not replace the existing attribute values, but to add a new set of attributes with the provided values. Here is sample of how we would use this method to update the attributes for multiple items with a single call to SimpleDB.

```
>>> import boto
>>>
>>> sdb_connection = boto.connect_sdb()
>>>
>>> songs_domain = sdb_connection.get_domain('songs')
>>>
>>> print songs_domain.name
songs
>>>
>>> for item in songs_domain.select("SELECT * FROM `songs` WHERE Song='My
Way' OR Song='Transmission'"):
...     print ">>",item.name,item
...
>> 112222222 {u'Rating': [u'****', u'Excellent', u'4 stars'], u'Artist':
u'Frank Sinatra', u'FileKey': u'b194a34e3340bc1e7df4e8b92a6b95d3',
u'Song': u'My Way', u'FileName': u'My Way.mp3', u'Year': u'2002',
u'Genre': u'Easy Listening'}
>>>

>> 6767969119 {u'Rating': [u'Excellent', u'*****'], u'Artist': u'Joy
Division', u'FileKey': u'5e0c3a6fae1dda6aaf6ae32506d41208', u'Song':
u'Transmission', u'FileName': u'Transmission.mp3', u'Year': u'1981',
u'Genre': u'Alternative'}
>>>
>>> update_data = {'112222222': {'Year':'2009'}, '6767969119':
{'Genre':'Rock'}}
>>>
```

```
>>> songs_domain.batch_put_attributes(update_data, True)
True
>>>
>>> for item in songs_domain.select("SELECT * FROM `songs` WHERE Song='My
Way' OR Song='Transmission'"):
...     print ">>",item.name,item
...
>> 112222222 {u'Rating': [u'****', u'Excellent', u'4 stars'], u'Artist':
u'Frank Sinatra', u'FileKey': u'b194a34e3340bc1e7df4e8b92a6b95d3',
u'Song': u'My Way', u'FileName': u'My Way.mp3', u'Year': u'2009',
u'Genre': u'Easy Listening'}

>> 6767969119 {u'Rating': [u'Excellent', u'*****'], u'Artist': u'Joy
Division', u'FileKey': u'5e0c3a6fae1dda6aaf6ae32506d41208', u'Song':
u'Transmission', u'FileName': u'Transmission.mp3', u'Year': u'1981',
u'Genre': u'Rock'}
>>>
>>>
```

In this section, we looked at how to make a single call to SimpleDB and update the attributes for multiple items using Java, PHP, or Python.

 The `BatchPutAttributes` operation succeeds or fails in its entirety. There are no partial puts.

Be aware when using this operation with the HTTP GET method, as you can easily exceed the maximum URL size when making a REST request.

SimpleDB currently enforces the following limitations for this operation:

- 256 attribute name-value pairs per item
- 1 MB request size
- 1 billion attributes per domain
- 10 GB of total user data storage per domain
- 25 item limit per `BatchPutAttributes` operation

Serialized SimpleDB requests

In the previous section, we used a batch operation for updating multiple items in a single call. This will work just fine as long as you only need to update up to 25 items at a time. What if you need to update 1000 items, or even 100,000 items? You can certainly use the simple batch operation, but making the requests one after the other serially will seriously degrade your performance and slow your application down. Here is a simple Python script that updates items by making three different calls to SimpleDB, but in a serial fashion, that is one call after another. You can run this script with the time command on Unix/Linux/Mac OS X to get the execution time. This will give us a baseline to look at when we convert this same script into using parallel operations.

Running this through time on my laptop shows the following output:

```
Updated items for domain 'Domain:songs' to : {'112222222': {'Year':
'2010'}, '6767969119': {'Genre': ''}}

Updated items for domain 'Domain:songs' to : {'112222222': {'Year':
'2001'}, '6767969119': {'Genre': 'Alternative'}}

Updated items for domain 'Domain:songs' to : {'112222222': {'Year':
'2010'}, '6767969119': {'Genre': 'Pop'}}


real    0m3.184s

user    0m0.092s

sys     0m0.066s
```

The time command gives you the following information:

- real: The elapsed real time between invocation and termination
- user: The user CPU time
- sys: The system CPU time

For our purposes, we can use the real time, which is the actual elapsed time. So running this simple update serially took about 3.184 seconds. Now let's see if we can speed that up.

Parallelizing SimpleDB requests

We can take advantage of the excellent support for concurrency available in SimpleDB by parallelizing our batch requests by multi-threading or using multiple processes to make requests in parallel. There are several different ways of parallelizing our requests using Python. We will look at the different ways of doing this in Python. We will be using the batch operation as an example to illustrate each threading example, but you can apply these principles with any of the SimpleDB operations:

- Inserting items
- Deleting items
- Updating items

Parallelizing SimpleDB requests in Java

Java provides excellent support within the language for running operations concurrently. In this section, we will use the `java.util.concurrent` package to see how easy it is to insert multiple items concurrently into SimpleDB by using a `threadpool`. Recent versions of Java provide a `ThreadPoolExecutor` class that has all of the functionality that we need for our purpose. We will first instantiate a `ThreadPoolExecutor` and provide a variety of configuration options to it such as the minimum size of the pool, a handler class that is executed in case the task being performed is rejected, and so on. Anytime that we need to run something in a different thread, we invoke the `execute()` method on our `ThreadPoolExecutor` object and provide it an object that implements the `Runnable` interface and performs the actual task. That's all there is to it. In this example, we will create a simple `SongsWorker` class that implements the `Runnable` interface and does the actual updating of an item's attributes. The example is bit contrived and deliberately kept simple so that the concept is clear. Here is a sample Java class that performs update of attributes by using threads.

```
package simpledbbook;

import com.xerox.amazonws.sdb.Item;
import com.xerox.amazonws.sdb.Domain;
import com.xerox.amazonws.sdb.ItemAttribute;
import com.xerox.amazonws.sdb.QueryWithAttributesResult;
import com.xerox.amazonws.sdb.SDBException;
import com.xerox.amazonws.sdb.SimpleDB;
import java.util.ArrayList;
import java.util.HashMap;
import java.util.Iterator;
```

```
import java.util.List;
import java.util.Map;
import java.util.concurrent.ArrayBlockingQueue;
import java.util.concurrent.RejectedExecutionHandler;
import java.util.concurrent.ThreadPoolExecutor;
import java.util.concurrent.TimeUnit;
import java.util.logging.Level;
import java.util.logging.Logger;
public class ThreadedSongs {
    private static Domain domain = null;

    private static class UpdateWorker implements Runnable {
        Map<String, List<ItemAttribute>> attrItemMap = null;

        public UpdateWorker(Map<String, List<ItemAttribute>>
            attrItemMap) {
            this.attrItemMap = attrItemMap;
        }

        public void run() {
            try {
                domain.batchPutAttributes(attrItemMap);
            } catch (SDBException ex) {
                Logger.getLogger(ThreadedSongs.class.getName())
                .log(Level.SEVERE, null, ex);
            }
        }
    }

    public static void main(String[] args) {
        SimpleDB sdb = new SimpleDB(awsAccessId, awsSecretKey, true);
        try {
            domain = sdb.getDomain("songs");
            String queryString = "SELECT * FROM `songs`
                WHERE `Song`='My Way' OR `Song`='Transmission'";
            System.out.println("Items before threaded update
                ************");
            String nextToken = null;
            do {
                QueryWithAttributesResult queryResults =
                    domain.selectItems(queryString, nextToken);
                Map<String, List<ItemAttribute>> items = queryResults
                    .getItems();
                for (String id : items.keySet()) {
                    System.out.println("Item : " + id);
                    for (ItemAttribute attr : items.get(id)) {
```

```
                    System.out.println(attr.getName() + " = "
                        + attr.getValue());
                }
            }
            nextToken = queryResults.getNextToken();
        } while (nextToken != null &&
            !nextToken.trim().equals(""));

        ThreadPoolExecutor pool = null;

        pool = new ThreadPoolExecutor(20, 30, 5,
            TimeUnit.SECONDS,
            new ArrayBlockingQueue<Runnable>(10));
        pool.setRejectedExecutionHandler(new
            RejectedExecutionHandler() {

            public void rejectedExecution(Runnable r,
                ThreadPoolExecutor executor) {
                // Failed. You can retry this op again if you like
                    System.err.println("Failed to update item");
            }
        });

        List<Map<String, List<ItemAttribute>>>
            itemsToUpdate = new ArrayList<Map<String,
            List<ItemAttribute>>>();
        List<ItemAttribute> list = new
            ArrayList<ItemAttribute>();
        list.add(new ItemAttribute("Year", "2009", true));
        list.add(new ItemAttribute("Genre", "Soundtrack", true));
        Map<String, List<ItemAttribute>> attrItemMap = new
            HashMap<String, List<ItemAttribute>>();
        attrItemMap.put("112222222", list);
        itemsToUpdate.add(attrItemMap);

        list = new ArrayList<ItemAttribute>();
        list.add(new ItemAttribute("Year", "2010", true));
        list.add(new ItemAttribute("Genre", "Dance", true));
        attrItemMap = new HashMap<String, List<ItemAttribute>>();
        attrItemMap.put("6767969119", list);
        itemsToUpdate.add(attrItemMap);

        Iterator<Map<String, List<ItemAttribute>>>
            updateIter = itemsToUpdate.iterator();
        while (updateIter.hasNext()) {
            pool.execute(new UpdateWorker(updateIter.next()));
        }

        long sleeptime = 5000L;
        System.out.println("");
```

```
System.out.println("Sleeping for 5 seconds after the
    update. Ah! Eventual Consistency ...");
try {
    Thread.sleep(sleeptime);
} catch (InterruptedException e) {
    e.printStackTrace();
}
System.out.println("");
System.out.println("Items after threaded update
    ************");
do {
    QueryWithAttributesResult queryResults = domain
        .selectItems(queryString, nextToken);
    Map<String, List<ItemAttribute>> items = queryResults
        .getItems();
    for (String id : items.keySet()) {
        System.out.println("Item : " + id);
        for (ItemAttribute attr : items.get(id)) {
            System.out.println(attr.getName() + " = "
            + attr.getValue());
        }
    }
    nextToken = queryResults.getNextToken();
} while (nextToken != null && !nextToken
    .trim().equals(""));
} catch (SDBException ex) {
    System.out.println(ex.getMessage());
}
}
}
```

Parallelizing SimpleDB requests in PHP

None of the available PHP APIs for SimpleDB support multi-curl for parallel requests.

Parallelizing SimpleDB requests in Python

In this section, we will explore different methods for parallelizing our requests to SimpleDB using Python.

Simple threading

We can use Python's built-in threading support and make parallel requests to SimpleDB. Here is a simple Python script that uses the `threading` module.

```python
#!/usr/bin/env python

import threading
import boto


class ThreadedBatchPut(threading.Thread):

  def __init__(self,domain_name, update_data):
    threading.Thread.__init__(self)
    sdb = boto.connect_sdb()
    self.domain = sdb.get_domain(domain_name)
    self.data_to_update = update_data

  def run(self):
    self.domain.batch_put_attributes(self.data_to_update)
    print "Updated items for domain '%s' to : %s" % (self.domain, self.
data_to_update)


def main():

  '''This is the data that you are updating in SimpleDB.
  We have kept this simple so as to clarify the concept'''
  data_to_be_updated = [{'112222222': {'Year':'2010'}, '6767969119':
{'Genre':''}},{'112222222': {'Year':'2001'}, '6767969119': {'Genre':'Alte
rnative'}},{'112222222': {'Year':'2010'}, '6767969119': {'Genre':'Pop'}}]


  for i in data_to_be_updated:
    t = ThreadedBatchPut('songs',i)
    t.start()

main()
```

We create a subclass from the Thread class, and construct it by providing the name of the domain along with the data to be updated. When the thread actually runs, it will use the domain object created in the constructor and use the batch operation to update the items. You can start as many threads as there are items to be updated. The data_to_be_updated variable that you see in the script is an array of dictionaries. Each item within this array will be processed within one thread. Each item is of course a dictionary that has the items to be updated. Keep in mind that the 25 item limit for the batch operation means that each of the dictionaries in this array can only contain a maximum of 25 items.

> SimpleDB makes multiple copies of your data and uses an eventual consistency update model. An immediate Get or Select request (read) after a Put or Delete request might not return the updated data. Some items might be updated before others, despite the fact that the operation never partially succeeds.

Here is the output when we run the simple threading sample.

```
Updated items for domain 'Domain:songs' to : {'112222222': {'Year':
'2010'}, '6767969119': {'Genre': ''}}

Updated items for domain 'Domain:songs' to : {'112222222': {'Year':
'2001'}, '6767969119': {'Genre': 'Alternative'}}

Updated items for domain 'Domain:songs' to : {'112222222': {'Year':
'2010'}, '6767969119': {'Genre': 'Pop'}}


real    0m1.294s

user    0m0.090s

sys     0m0.057s
```

As you can see, we have significantly reduced the time, down to 1.294s. You can see such an improvement when just using a small set for our tests, but a large dataset will show you even more advantages of using parallel operations to optimize SimpleDB operations.

Threading with queues

The pattern we used earlier of simple threading works, but can be a bit of a pain to program when you need to share any resources. The nicer way to use threads in Python would be to use queues and threading together. Here is the same code sample rewritten now to use a queue:

```python
#!/usr/bin/env python
import Queue
import threading
import boto

queue = Queue.Queue()
class QueuedBatchPut(threading.Thread):
  def __init__(self, queue, domain_name):
    threading.Thread.__init__(self)
    sdb = boto.connect_sdb()
    self.queue = queue
    self.domain = sdb.get_domain(domain_name)

  def run(self):
    while True:
      data_to_update = self.queue.get()
      self.domain.batch_put_attributes(data_to_update)
      print "Updated items for domain '%s' to : %s" % (self.domain,
data_to_update)
      self.queue.task_done()

def main():
  '''This is the data that you are updating in SimpleDB.
  We have kept this simple so as to clarify the concept'''
  data_to_be_updated = [{'112222222': {'Year':'2010'}, '6767969119':
{'Genre':''}},{'112222222': {'Year':'2001'}, '6767969119': {'Gen
re':'Alternative'}},{'112222222': {'Year':'2010'}, '6767969119':
{'Genre':'Pop'}}]

  '''Create a pool of threads and provide each thread with the queue
and the name of the domain'''
  for i in range(len(data_to_be_updated)):
    t = QueuedBatchPut(queue, 'songs')
    t.setDaemon(True)
    t.start()

  '''Populate the queue with your data to be updated'''
  for i in data_to_be_updated:
    queue.put (i)
```

```
    '''You have to wait until the queue is done processing'''
    queue.join()

main()
```

This is a commonly used pattern for threaded programming in Python. We first create an instance of the `Queue` class. We then create a pool of threads, with each instance of the new `QueuedBatchPut` class, which subclasses `Thread` and does the actual update of values in SimpleDB. We put all our work data on to the queue. The pool of threads picks up items off the queue and processes them. Each thread picks up one item that is one unit of work or one batch of items to be updated, and updates the values appropriately on SimpleDB. Once the piece of work is done, a signal is sent to the queue notifying it that the task is complete. The main program waits till the queue is completely empty and then exits the program.

Running the queued sample with `time` gives us the following output:

```
Updated items for domain 'Domain:songs' to : {'112222222': {'Year':
'2010'}, '6767969119': {'Genre': 'Pop'}}

Updated items for domain 'Domain:songs' to : {'112222222': {'Year':
'2001'}, '6767969119': {'Genre': 'Alternative'}}

Updated items for domain 'Domain:songs' to : {'112222222': {'Year':
'2010'}, '6767969119': {'Genre': ''}}


real    0m1.443s
user    0m0.090s
sys     0m0.054s
```

Still much better, but slightly slower than the simple threading sample. This could also be due to some network latency, but the clarity gained by using queues and decreased programming complexity is well worth the difference.

Threading with workerpool

There is an open source project named **workerpool** that encapsulates some of the thread pool pattern, and makes it easy to work with threading and jobs in Python. In this section, we will use workerpool to rewrite our sample. You can either download it from `http://code.google.com/p/workerpool/`, or you can use Python setup tools to install the egg package for this software. You can install the egg version from the command line as follows:

```
$ easy_install workerpool
```

Here is the same sample rewritten to take advantage of workerpool library.
It is a bit cleaner and simpler than using the queues directly within your code.

```python
#!/usr/bin/env python
import workerpool
import boto

class WorkerpoolBatchPut(workerpool.Job):
  def __init__(self,domain_name, data_to_update):

    sdb = boto.connect_sdb()
    self.domain = sdb.get_domain(domain_name)
    self.data_to_update = data_to_update

  def run(self):
      self.domain.batch_put_attributes(self.data_to_update)
      print "Updated items for domain '%s' to : %s" % (self.domain,
self.data_to_update)

def main():

  '''This is the data that you are updating in SimpleDB.
  We have kept this simple so as to clarify the concept'''
  data_to_be_updated = [{'112222222': {'Year':'2010'}, '6767969119':
{'Genre':''}},{'112222222': {'Year':'2001'}, '6767969119': {'Gen
re':'Alternative'}},{'112222222': {'Year':'2010'}, '6767969119':
{'Genre':'Pop'}}]

  pool = workerpool.WorkerPool(size=len(data_to_be_updated))

  '''Create a job and put it on the pool'''
  for i in data_to_be_updated:
    job = WorkerpoolBatchPut('songs', i)
    pool.put(job)


  '''You have to wait until all jobs are done'''
  pool.shutdown()
  pool.wait()


main()
```

Here is the output when running the workerpool sample with time.

```
Updated items for domain 'Domain:songs' to : {'112222222': {'Year':
'2010'}, '6767969119': {'Genre': ''}}

Updated items for domain 'Domain:songs' to : {'112222222': {'Year':
'2001'}, '6767969119': {'Genre': 'Alternative'}}

Updated items for domain 'Domain:songs' to : {'112222222': {'Year':
'2010'}, '6767969119': {'Genre': 'Pop'}}
```

```
real    0m1.487s
user    0m0.096s
sys     0m0.062s
```

Once again, it takes almost as much time as the sample that uses the queues. These are two similar ways of using threading, and you can use whichever is better suited to your programming style.

Concurrency and SimpleDB

The power of SimpleDB becomes truly apparent when you start taking advantage of the support for concurrency by writing multithreaded programs for interacting with it. You can choose the SimpleDB operation that you like—inserting items, deleting items, updating items, and easily scale it up using **boto** and the parallelization techniques that we looked at in this chapter.

There are some things that you really need to be aware of when using concurrency with SimpleDB:

- If you make a large number of concurrent SimpleDB calls, it can sometimes result in Service Unavailable (503) responses from SimpleDB. Your application must be aware of this fact and handle this by retrying the request with an exponential back-off.

- Here is a blog post that argues a position opposite from the above and makes a good case why using exponential back-off is not a good strategy when performing concurrent operations on SimpleDB—http://www.daemonology.net/blog/2008-06-29-high-performance-simpledb.html.

- The network latency can really affect your results even when you are parallelizing operations, if you are running outside Amazon's virtual environment. If your application is running on EC2, the calls to SimpleDB across Amazon's internal network are blazing fast! This reduced latency in combination with parallelization will give your SimpleDB a real boost. There have also been some reports that Amazon enforces a limit of 500 BatchPut operations per minute in order to ensure a good quality of service for all customers. This is a great reason for utilizing partitioning for your domains, even in cases when the domain does not exceed the 10 GB limit.

The samples in this chapter use `BatchPutAttributes` to illustrate techniques for running parallel operations against SimpleDB. You can apply the same technique to other SimpleDB operations, such as insert and delete.

Summary

In this chapter, we discussed utilizing multiple threads for running parallel operations against SimpleDB in Java, PHP, and Python in order to speed up processing times and taking advantage of the excellent support for concurrency in SimpleDB.

Applications require a database that can adapt as the user community grows. SimpleDB can support this in a cost-effective way, as long as the developer is willing to learn a new database paradigm. As developers, we dream of creating software that catches the public's fancy and goes viral. Ten users today, 50,000 tomorrow. What a wonderful problem to have!

Index

BoxUsage
- about 62, 167
- costs, computing 168
- hypothetical cost, computing 169
- Java 172
- machine utilization in EU region, costs computing 169
- machine utilization in US region, costs computing 168
- PHP 175
- Python 178
- usage reports 169-172
- value 167

BoxUsage, in Java
- about 172, 173
- Select, cost 173, 174

BoxUsage, in PHP
- about 175
- domain creation, cost 177, 178
- items creation, cost 178
- NextToken, cost 175, 176
- Select, cost 177

BoxUsage, in Python 178-180

buckets, S3
- about 142
- naming, requisites 142

C

Cache_Lite
- about 193
- with SimpleDB, using in PHP 197-200

caching
- about 184
- with SimpleDB, logic flow 193, 194

comparison operators
- != 119
- < 119
- <= 119
- = 119
- > 119
- >= 119
- about 119
- between 120
- every() 120
- In 120
- is not null 120

- is null 120
- like 120
- not like 120

concurrency
- and SimpleDB 223

Conditional Put/Delete 82-84

Consistent Read
- for getAttributes and Select 79-81

Coordinated Universal Time. *See* UTC times

COUNT() 135

cPanel Linux servers
- Cache_Lite, installing 193

createDomain() method 29

D

data, from memcached
- retrieving, in Java 190
- retrieving, in PHP 191, 192
- retrieving, in Python 192, 193
- storing, in Java 190
- storing, in PHP 191, 192
- storing, in Python 192, 193

data model, SimpleDB 57

DataUtils class 88

date values
- storing 91, 92
- storing, with Java 93
- storing, with PHP 93, 94
- storing, with Python 94

decode_b64_value() method 100

decode_datetime() method 94

decodeNum function 89

delete_attributes method 61

deleteAttributes method 59

deleteDomain method 59

delete_item method 61

deleteItem method 58

domain constraints, SimpleDB 67

domain metadata
- components 66
- retrieving, with Java 63, 64
- retrieving, with PHP 64
- retrieving, with Python 64, 65

domainMetadata method 59

O

OR operator 132

P

partitioning 180, 181
partitioning, SimpleDB 180, 181
PEAR 193
PHP
  about 31, 32
  additional metadata, creating 151
  attributes 74
  base64 values, using 99
  BatchPutAttributes 209, 210
  Boolean values, storing 95, 96
  BoxUsage 175
  Cache_Lite, using with SimpleDB 197-200
  data, retrieving from memcached 191, 192
  data, storing from memcached 191, 192
  data values, storing 93, 94
  domain, creating 35, 59
  domain, deleting 37
  domains, listing 35
  files, retrieving from S3 162, 163
  getAttributes 137
  items, manipulating 35, 36
  memcached client 189
  multiple values, storing in single
      attribute 77
  numeric values, storing 89
  S3 bucket, creating 147
  sample data, importing 106
  SimpleDB, exploring 32-35
  SimpleDB keys, setting 34
  SimpleDB requests, parallelizing 217
  SimpleDB, sample programs 33
  simple predicate query 118, 119
  simple Select query 113, 115
  songs, uploading to S3 155-159
PHP Extensions and Applications Reposi-
    tory. See PEAR
PHP library
  batchPutAttributes method 59
  deleteAttributes method 59
  deleteDomain method 59
  domainMetadata method 59

getAttributes method 59
listDomains method 59
methods 59
putAttributes method 59
select method 59
predicates, Select expression
  about 117
  simple predicate query, with Java 117, 118
  simple predicate query, with PHP 118, 119
  simple predicate query, with Python 119
pricing, S3 143, 144
putAttributes function 200, 209
put_attributes method 61
putAttributes method 59
Python
  about 37
  additional metadata, creating 151-154
  attributes 75
  base64 values, using 100
  BatchPutAttributes 211, 212
  Boolean values, storing 96, 97
  boto 38
  BoxUsage 178, 179
  data, retrieving from memcached 192, 193
  data, storing from memcached 192, 193
  data values, storing 94
  domain, creating 40, 59, 61
  domain, retrieving 40, 41
  files, retrieving from S3 163, 164
  getAttributes 139
  items, creating 40, 41
  items, deleting 42
  memcached client 189, 190
  memcached, using with SimpleDB 201-203
  multiple values, storing in single
      attribute 78
  numeric values, storing 90, 91
  S3 bucket, creating 147, 148
  sample data, importing 109, 110
  SimpleDB, exploring 39
  SimpleDB requests, parallelizing 217
  simple predicate query 119
  simple Select query 115
  songs, uploading to S3 160, 161

Thank you for buying
Amazon SimpleDB Developer Guide

About Packt Publishing

Packt, pronounced 'packed', published its first book "Mastering phpMyAdmin for Effective MySQL Management" in April 2004 and subsequently continued to specialize in publishing highly focused books on specific technologies and solutions.

Our books and publications share the experiences of your fellow IT professionals in adapting and customizing today's systems, applications, and frameworks. Our solution based books give you the knowledge and power to customize the software and technologies you're using to get the job done. Packt books are more specific and less general than the IT books you have seen in the past. Our unique business model allows us to bring you more focused information, giving you more of what you need to know, and less of what you don't.

Packt is a modern, yet unique publishing company, which focuses on producing quality, cutting-edge books for communities of developers, administrators, and newbies alike. For more information, please visit our website: www.packtpub.com.

About Packt Enterprise

In 2010, Packt launched two new brands, Packt Enterprise and Packt Open Source, in order to continue its focus on specialization. This book is part of the Packt Enterprise brand, home to books published on enterprise software – software created by major vendors, including (but not limited to) IBM, Microsoft and Oracle, often for use in other corporations. Its titles will offer information relevant to a range of users of this software, including administrators, developers, architects, and end users.

Writing for Packt

We welcome all inquiries from people who are interested in authoring. Book proposals should be sent to author@packtpub.com. If your book idea is still at an early stage and you would like to discuss it first before writing a formal book proposal, contact us; one of our commissioning editors will get in touch with you.

We're not just looking for published authors; if you have strong technical skills but no writing experience, our experienced editors can help you develop a writing career, or simply get some additional reward for your expertise.

Oracle VM Manager 2.1.2

ISBN: 978-1-847197-12-2   Paperback: 244 pages

Manage a Flexible and Elastic Data Center with Oracle VM Manager

1. Learn quickly to install Oracle VM Manager and Oracle VM Servers

2. Learn to manage your Virtual Data Center using Oracle VM Manager

3. Import VMs from the Web, template, repositories, and other VM formats such as VMware

4. Learn powerful Xen Hypervisor utilities such as xm, xentop, and virsh

Oracle Coherence 3.5

ISBN: 978-1-847196-12-5   Paperback: 408 pages

Create Internet-scale applications using Oracle's high-performance data grid

1. Build scalable web sites and Enterprise applications using a market-leading data grid product

2. Design and implement your domain objects to work most effectively with Coherence and apply Domain Driven Designs (DDD) to Coherence applications

3. Leverage Coherence events and continuous queries to provide real-time updates to client applications

Please check **www.PacktPub.com** for information on our titles

IBM WebSphere eXtreme Scale 6

ISBN: 978-1-847197-44-3   Paperback: 292 pages

Build scalable, high-performance software with IBM's data grid

1. Get hands-on experience with eXtreme Scale APIs, and understand the different approaches to using data grids

2. Introduction to new design patterns for both eXtreme Scale and data grids in general

3. Tutorial-style guide through the major data grid features and libraries

4. Start working with a data grid through code samples and clear walkthroughs

High Availability MySQL Cookbook

ISBN: 978-1-847199-94-2   Paperback: 264 pages

Over 60 simple but incredibly effective recipes focusing on different methods of achieving high availability for MySQL database

1. Analyze and learn different high availability options, including clustering and replication solutions within MySQL

2. Improve uptime of your MySQL databases with simple recipes showing powerful high availability techniques for MySQL

3. Tune your MySQL database for optimal performance.

4. The only complete, practical, book of MySQL high availability techniques and tools on the market

Please check **www.PacktPub.com** for information on our titles

www.ingramcontent.com/pod-product-compliance
Lightning Source LLC
Chambersburg PA
CBHW060540060326
40690CB00017B/3555